SPIRITUAL
WARFARE
and
DELIVERANCE

SPIRITUAL WARFARE

and

DELIVERANCE

HOW TO MINISTER TO THE DEMONICALLY OPPRESSED AND POSSESSED

HAROLD RISTAU

BakerBooks

a division of Baker Publishing Group
Grand Rapids, Michigan

Published by Baker Books
a division of Baker Publishing Group
Grand Rapids, Michigan
BakerBooks.com

Printed in the United States of America

Library of Congress Cataloging-in-Publication Data
Names: Ristau, Harold, author.
Title: Spiritual warfare and deliverance : how to minister to the demonically oppressed and possessed / Harold Ristau.
Description: Grand Rapids, Michigan : Baker Books, a division of Baker Publishing Group, [2025] | Includes bibliographical references.
Identifiers: LCCN 2024052046 | ISBN 9781540904393 (paperback) | ISBN 9781540904928 (casebound) | ISBN 9781493450398 (ebook)
Subjects: LCSH: Spiritual warfare. | Demoniac possession. | Exorcism.
Classification: LCC BV4509.5 .R52 2025 | DDC 235/.4—dc23/eng/20250203
LC record available at https://lccn.loc.gov/2024052046

Cover design by David Carlson, Gearbox

Baker Publishing Group publications use paper produced from sustainable forestry practices and postconsumer waste whenever possible.

25   26   27   28   29   30   31   7   6   5   4   3   2   1

To my dear wife, Elise,
for supporting and encouraging me
during twenty-five years of challenges
in a peculiar pastoral ministry

CONTENTS

INTRODUCTION

If you're skeptical about the existence of demons, you won't benefit much from this book. Sure, your curiosity may be satisfied a little bit. But other than that, you're wasting your time. The prejudice of the skeptical blinds them from detecting the extraordinary when they look at the world around them. After all, as C. S. Lewis implies in *The Screwtape Letters*, it's in the devil's best interest to go undercover in a "scientific" society filled with lukewarm, unbelieving Christians.

Satan doesn't want to tempt people to believe in him. Too many bizarre displays of evil—like house hauntings or demon possessions—may drive petrified people to prayer, or to the Church, which is Lucifer's worst nightmare. Casting doubt on the real threat he poses is this enemy's best line of attack. Caricatures of demons as comical, mythological cartoons help. They offer an effective deterrent to taking Satan seriously. Only crazy people believe in the devil, right? No wonder many Christian denominations are so embarrassed by the idea of hell and the devil that they do everything they can to avoid these subjects entirely.

In the developing world, the mood is different. Virtually everybody believes in the supernatural; in such places, the devil takes a more straightforward approach and has two strategies. Either he seeks to convince people he is good and useful to them, or he tries to frighten them into believing he is stronger than the true God. So you better do what he wants. And if you don't, he'll make you pay.

Take voodoo, for example. In one of the poorest countries in the Western Hemisphere, Haiti, occultism is used as a tool to increase personal power. "Pacts with the devil" impact business deals, drive government decisions, and help avenge the crimes of your enemies. Of course, this all results in an amplification of pain and suffering in everybody's lives. But when your heart tells you that you deserve more from life, and the world tells you that you need to look out for number one, short-term gain and temporal pleasures can seem pretty attractive. Most Haitians believe in God and the devil. They're just not sure which is the more beneficial of the two. These syncretistic Christians know God is omnipotent, but they're unsure whether He actually cares about them. They don't believe He is Love. They often live in desperation. Where true faith is lacking, fear of the future, economic frustration, and psychological depression are ammunition for a devil who isn't shy in flaunting his services. Ouija, mediums, fortune tellers, diviners, necromancers, astrologers, and the like can actually do what they claim. Certainly, there are always swindlers and showmen, but there's also the real deal.

Yet even frauds can ruin the lives of those who believe in them.

Avoiding the Occult

A family friend of mine paid to have her palm read. The woman told her that her son would die a violent death. The tragedy never occurred. Yet the mother lived her life in terror and overprotected her child, who resented her until the day she died. The devilish lie had a huge consequence on the unfolding of her life.

As a young boy, I was exposed to a slew of inappropriate TV and media. It took me years to recover from the spiritual damage. Whether a monster lived in my closet made little difference to the nefarious scars left on my developing mind. Today, as a father of five, I wish I had practiced more parental censorship and boycotting of films when my kids were young. Movies are a powerful source of information. Horror movies tend to either overstate the power of demons by making us believe the devil has the upper hand over the Lord or understate them by treating the subject as sheer comedy.

In any case, when it comes to the charlatans, God's Word is uncompromising:

> Then I will draw near to you for judgment. I will be a swift witness against the sorcerers, against the adulterers, against those who swear falsely, against those who oppress the hired worker in his wages, the widow and the fatherless, against those who thrust aside the sojourner, and do not fear me, says the LORD of hosts. (Mal. 3:5)

Whether it is real or fake, one ought to avoid the occult at all costs. When it comes to legitimate satanic arts, like Saul invoking the spirit of Samuel from the dead (1 Sam. 28:7), the Lord says: "And when they say to you, 'Inquire of the mediums and the necromancers who chirp and mutter,' should not a people inquire of their God? Should they inquire of the dead on behalf of the living?" (Isa. 8:19). Witches may succeed in calling up the dead or raise demons that appear as human personages, but the fact that "it works" by no means suggests that it's a good thing! Although the "magicians" in Egypt were no match for the miraculous power of God's servants—Moses's pole-turned-snake easily consumed Pharaoh's serpents—true demonic powers were still being employed by the occult practitioners.

African tribes in which witchcraft maintains a cultural footing habitually put curses on their neighbors to gain power over them. Ancient formulas for "blessings" and curses are customary among many Indigenous religious communities. I knew a Roman Catholic priest and missionary who discovered he had been cursed. It was easily dealt with by prayer and Christian ministry. Nevertheless, for months he was mystified by a heightened sense of demonic activity in his life.

In North America, the occult is increasingly popular. Christians here have been lulled to sleep when it comes to the threat of the occult, but Satanism is alive and well and even normalized in secular circles among the rich and powerful.[1] Disenchanted youth are drawn to witchcraft due to the insecurities that come with growing up. Teenagers want information that they aren't supposed to have. Information is power. They want increased control in their lives. My high school English teacher used to loan out Ouija boards during the lunch hour to help build up the self-esteem of insecure students. And that was thirty-five years ago.

I once worked with a socially awkward and reclusive young man who joined the Masonic Lodge because he wanted friends. His thirst for popularity led him to invite a spirit guide into his life, a demon disguised as an "angel of light"

1. See, for example, Paul Bond, "Satan Is Getting Hot as Hell in American Pop Culture," *Newsweek*, March 28, 2023, https://www.newsweek.com/satan-getting-hot-hell-american-pop-culture-1790669; Damian Thompson, "Inside America's Satanist movement," *The Spectator*, April 29, 2023, https://www.spectator.co.uk/article/inside-americas-satanist-movement/.

(2 Cor. 11:14). He viewed the entity as an altruistic and amiable life coach. Well, this wicked creature messed him up terribly. How? He used this loathsome entity to spy on his neighbors.

The results of this man's obsession with this invisible friend? He started to view others with such suspicion and jealousy that all his relationships began to fall apart. He became a paranoid basket case. He didn't gain more control over his life but less. And it's a lot harder to get rid of these evil pests than to attract them. Whereas the Holy Spirit is a gentleman and won't stay where He isn't welcome, when you open the door to the devil, even a crack, he shoves his beastly foot there and forces it open with all his might. Sadly, most people make it easy for this intruder. They inadvertently invite him in. So one of the major entry points for demons into our hearts, souls, and lives is through the door of the occult.

A Changing World

Western society is changing, and the devil's tactics are not as covert as they used to be. We have allowed ourselves to become more spiritually vulnerable to him. With the demise of the Church as a governing influence in our world and the decline of devoted Christians as spiritual warriors comes a stronger dose of demonic attack around the globe. Although we are saved by grace alone, spiritually lazy Christians need to take heed of the Lord's warning: "Nevertheless, when the Son of Man comes, will he find faith on earth?" (Luke 18:8).

In fairness to those who think these warnings are sensationalistic or overly dramatic, it's difficult to empirically determine whether demonism is on the rise or whether today's technology has simply heightened our awareness of what has always been present. With faster and easier ways of accessing information at our fingertips, we are more informed and exposed to cases of demonic manifestation. In the past, we just didn't—because we couldn't—hear about it as much.

Yet based upon my observations throughout twenty-five years of ministry as a pastor, chaplain, and professor, I have a sneaking suspicion that things are indeed getting worse and true spirituality is becoming harder to come by; formerly solid church bodies continue to succumb to the temptations of doctrinal compromise. The number of phone calls and emails I receive from people seeking help when it comes to this field has quadrupled over the last few years. Jesus promised an escalation of devilish activity prior to His return. In those latter days, the New Testament describes, "evil people and impostors will go on from bad to worse, deceiving and being deceived" (2 Tim. 3:13). The end is always a day nearer, and the devil knows it. After shuddering at the idea (James 2:19), this wily serpent gets busy digging holes into our lives. Identifying them is our main defense. Only then can we address them with offensive warfare: the weapons of the Spirit gifted to us from the headquarters of our Lord's holy Church. For these will never fail us.

Warning

Most of the literature on demonism and exorcism borders on speculative philosophy at best or spiritual snuff at worst—an excuse to share ghost stories under the guise of offering spiritual lessons. For this reason, I've always been hesitant to present on the topic unless I feel the hearers are sincerely interested in navigating this field with Christian wisdom and maturity. Otherwise, you can easily step on a mine, making the whole battle worse. This book is intended for mature Christians, believers who want help in fighting the battle instead of watching from the sidelines. It's for those who want to make sure that when they face off with the devil, they don't do it in sloppy and harmful ways. This book gives these Christians insights into this world—using scriptural stories as well as personal and historical anecdotes and examples—by helping them decipher the devil at work in both the ordinary spiritual war, consisting largely of fighting against temptation to sin, and the extraordinary spiritual war, observed in cases of demonic oppression and possession.

This book isn't intended as a playbook for laypeople to perform exorcisms. Reading a book on medicine doesn't make anyone a doctor. Yet that knowledge and exposure can help that reader better support the field of medicine and the medical community. Likewise, by learning about the theory and practice behind, say, an exorcism—how and when it's done, the ins and outs, its considerations and symptoms—Christians can be better prepared for the attacks they experience themselves and witness in others. The lessons learned in this book include practical tools and steps to protect Christians from evil forces in others and equip them in their own personal battles.

1

MY LAST EXORCISM

My last exorcism was unexpected.

I didn't have my briefcase packed with my traditional tools of church rites: hymnal, stole, and cross. I just had the small pocket Bible I often carry with me and a crucifix necklace that I never take off. Of course, like every true Christian, I was equipped with two praying hands and a ton of Scriptures embedded in my memory.

Those last two items are the most important when it comes to this unique ministry. The devil deploys all kinds of clever distractions. When our eyes begin to fail, our hands start to shake, and our mind loses focus, "the Spirit helps us in our weakness. For we do not know what to pray for as we ought, but the Spirit himself intercedes for us with groanings too deep for words" (Rom. 8:26).

I was visiting some colleagues at work when a man I had never met before asked to speak with me in private. Let's call him Frank.[1] Frank had heard about me from a friend.

---

1. All names in this book are pseudonyms, and I have changed certain details in all the narratives in order to protect identities. Yet all the stories are factual.

He knew I was a pastor and that I had special expertise in matters pertaining to the demonic realm.

Frank was quite candid and opened up to me immediately with all sorts of disturbing details about his life. He shared about an event in a house he had recently purchased at a good price, in which, he found out later, a murder had occurred. (I also found out, many years after the exorcism and after losing touch with Frank, that it had mysteriously burned down.) But in that house, Frank and his family experienced all sorts of supernatural activity, such as ghostly voices, frightening sounds, strange feelings, a reddish liquid dripping from the attic, and objects moving around by themselves.

The family pursued conventional strategies for coping with the strange phenomenon. They called the electrician, plumber, and family doctor. None of this helped.

Then, one morning, one of the children was found levitating in the kitchen.

It was clear that more radical action needed to be taken. Frank decided to confront the poltergeist head-on. He screamed and shouted at it. Then he challenged it to what can be best described as a wrestling match. It was a courageous yet stupid decision made by a desperate father and husband. After several rooms of the house had been trashed, he lost. Big surprise.

The result? The evil entity entered him. He wanted help but didn't know how to get it or where to go.

Demonism on the Rise

"Free popcorn at the haunted lighthouse" reads a poster for a Halloween event at a local attraction funded by the township every year. The advertisement continues with, "Come on out and talk to the friendly patron ghost, George, through Nancy our local medium."

Things sure have changed since I was a kid. Back then, satanic stuff was taboo. Churches told us to stay away from the dark arts and the occult. Now, some even encourage such alternative spiritualities. Yet as I mentioned in the introduction, I remember a hippie teacher at my high school who lent out Ouija boards at lunchtime. When I questioned this extracurricular activity, I remember him answering, "You should be more open-minded. The game works, you know."

It isn't about whether Ouija "works" but whether it's good. The world is deplorably confused about what is good and evil and knows little about the differences between angels and demons, blurring distinctions between God and the devil. After all, "the hour is coming when whoever kills you will think he is offering service to God" (John 16:2).

The accelerating tolerance, and even appetite, for evil things once considered dangerous isn't as surprising as you would think. How many parents take the time to inquire into what dark and disturbing content their kids are watching on the internet or the kinds of violent video games they're playing?

How many pastors turn a blind eye to suspicious activities in the lives of their church members? Some of us would rather remain ignorant of the dark secrets brewing within the families entrusted to our care. If we ask the touchy questions, we may need to act upon them. At best it's awkward. At worst it's petrifying.

Many Christians steer away from conversations that make people feel uneasy, including the subject of a real-life devil. Maybe it's due to all the normalized rhetoric about avoiding "negative energy" that sin is no longer mentioned from many pulpits. Christians seem to be fine talking about angels, but when it comes to demons, we'd rather change the subject. We praise the Lord for angelic miracles but remain hesitant to acknowledge the supernatural influences of the dark one.

Perhaps this imbalance stems from an uninformed faith in Christ as the conqueror of all evil. Yet inasmuch as the presence of sin, death, and the Old Adam in us is real, so are the activities of the devil.

The Lord Jesus conquered Satan on the D-day of Good Friday, but all creation still eagerly awaits the V-day victory parade at His second coming (Rom. 8:19).

We live between the times. So in the meantime, confessing demonic activity today doesn't betray a lack of faith in Christ's mighty power but rather is an acknowledgment that we straddle two conflicting worlds. The apostle Paul likens this struggle to a civil war between the sinner and saint status of every Christian: "So I find it to be a law that when I want to do right, evil lies close at hand" (Rom. 7:21).

Yet even here, God uses evil for His good purposes. Paul also shares how God used the devil in his life to humble his soul, helping him to better rely on the power and strength of Christ: "A thorn was given me in the flesh, a messenger of Satan to harass me, to keep me from becoming conceited" (2 Cor. 12:7). Christians shoot themselves in the foot when they deny the reality of evil, sin, and the devil. For how are we to defend ourselves in the battle if we ignore the threat? How can we be of loving service to our neighbors if, when demonic activity manifests itself in their lives and homes, we render unbiblical explanations and secularized excuses for such menacing spiritual phenomena?

Answering Skeptics

In my experience, skeptical North American Christians react in three ways to the notion of demonic oppression and possession, or, as some would call it, *demonism*.

One reaction interprets it as something limited to a faraway past. It may have been a reality in the days of the New Testament and the apostolic era, but certainly not today. These proponents carelessly treat accounts of present-day exorcism as shams and tend to view miracles and stories of angelic visits with suspicion. God is envisioned as a distant Creator, removed from the common events of our daily lives. Those who adhere to this idea tend to intellectualize their faith, theologizing about God at the expense of relating to Him in a personal way.

A second reaction accepts demonic activity as legitimate but dismisses it as a developing world problem. It still happens in places where missionaries haven't yet reached the unconverted with the gospel, but it's not something we need to worry about at home. "My life/family/church/neighborhood are safe, because we're good Christians." This really is ethnocentric snobbery. Certainly, the presence of the Holy Spirit is accentuated in any area inhabited by a great number of Christians. Christian culture is a good thing. But the devil is hard at work everywhere, especially among doubting, cultural, or lukewarm Christians who are as likely to join the devil's team as they are to remain with Jesus, whether they realize it or not.

The third reaction reduces the subject of demonism to psychology. When these brainwashed proponents witness displays of demonic possession or hear stories, they attribute it to psychological factors or offer other secular explanations. Sometimes, when they can't ignore the truth, they undergo cognitive dissonance and are unable to reconcile the internal contradiction of their unfounded disbelief with obvious reality.

Increase in Paranormal Activity

Yet with the increased visibility of paranormal activity, it's harder for the world to ignore the supernatural. I don't just mean the professionals who reduce demonism to the field of mental health but also those ascribing clear paranormal activity to material causes. The driving thrust of such parapsychology is attributing the paranormal to predispositions like ESP. They argue that some people are just able to harness a greater percentage of their brains, which allows them to do strange things. In other words, "mind over matter" explains some people's supernatural abilities to tell the future or move objects around without touching them. The secularist world relentlessly tries to confront spiritual phenomena in such worldly ways.

One noticeable difference between how true Christians and unbelievers approach this phenomenon of growing accounts of demonism is an angelizing of demons in the media. Once foes, demons are often now considered friends. Television shows like *Ghost Hunters* take a sympathetic approach to victimized spirits of the dead trapped in houses, having lost their way in the afterlife. Teenagers diagnosed with dissociative identity disorder boast on social media that their bodies are havens for spirits they can invoke at will, gladly embracing these demonic entities.[2] Traditional villains like Cruella de Vil or the Joker have been increasingly made the hero in blockbuster films. The bad guys aren't bad, they're just misunderstood.

Having swallowed the poison of postmodernity, we teach our children that evil is a question of relativity and context. Criminals aren't guilty because they're born that way. Good is evil, and evil is good. Witches aren't green crones with

---

2. Crystalie Matulewicz, "Embracing the Individuality of Alters in DID," *HealthyPlace*, December 3, 2015, https://www.healthyplace.com/blogs/dissociativeliving/2015/12/embracing-the-individuality-of-alters-in-did; Igor Jacob Pietkiewicz, Anna Bańbura-Nowak, Radoslaw Tomalski, and Suzette Boon, "Revisiting False-Positive and Imitated Dissociative Identity Disorder," *Frontier Psychology* 12 (May 2021), https://www.ncbi.nlm.nih.gov/pmc/articles/PMC8134744/.

long noses but beautiful, independent, modern women to which every little girl should aspire. The Rolling Stones no longer need to convince us to have "sympathy for the devil." We already do.

Yet when we adopt such revisionist and worldly approaches to the invisible realities that surround us, we cut ourselves off from the Lord's help and power. In our foolhardy denial, we make ourselves vulnerable to the evil one who assaults us without ceasing. "Woe to those who call evil good and good evil; who put darkness for light, and light for darkness" (Isa. 5:20).

Tools to Deal with the Devil

Because Christian clergy serve in the stead of Christ, demons either run or hide from these divine ambassadors who seek to expose and exterminate them. But demons remain under the spell of God's holy Word. Although there is no magic spell or formula for casting out demons, and each situation is unique, evil spirits are forced to react to the utterance of sacred phrases derived from the divine Scriptures.

The devil and his unholy hordes always remain under the authority of Christ, the Holy One of God. Like grabbing a worm when it peeks its head out of its hole, in my experience, exorcists have the ability to either yank a demon out or let it retreat.[3] And if they choose to pull, they need to be prepared for what they get: the slimy worm slithering around outside of the hole, in plain sight in all its ugliness, trying to make its way back and figure out what to do next.

---

3. Throughout this book, I define *exorcists* as skilled and experienced Christian practitioners of the ministry of deliverance in the case of demonic possessions.

If you are afraid of worms, you're in big trouble. I'm not scared, and it's not because I am courageous. It's because I have dealt with so many demons that I've found them to be powerless when handled in the right way. We're all afraid of the unfamiliar. And, of course, "perfect love casts out fear" (1 John 4:18). Jesus is that "perfect love."

There are some formulaic ways to deal with the devil; therefore, it's worthwhile learning the tools. But beware. The ministry of deliverance—confronting unusual levels of demonic presence in the lives of believers and unbelievers alike—is less of a science and more of an art. Each demon is different, and they don't all respond in the same way to Bible quotes, prayers, liturgies, or rebukes. Yet when you are in Christ, have faith, and speak words arising from the Holy Scriptures, you are well equipped.

I know this may all sound hard to believe. You may be skeptical. A lady once interrupted one of my presentations by shouting, "Do any of you people here actually believe this guy?" I remember a demon pointing to me in mockery and asking the same rhetorical question to a terror-stricken witness during one of my exorcisms: "Can you believe this f#@% pastor?"

Well, I can tell you it's all true, and if you don't believe me, read the Bible. The good news is that we are protected by Christ who works through His Holy Church and Word on earth. His holiness is a merciful shield around us as He prays for us: "Holy Father . . . My prayer is not that you take them out of the world but that you protect them from the evil one. . . . Sanctify them by the truth; your word is truth" (John 17:11, 15, 17 NIV).

Are you ready for the truth?

2

FRANK'S DELIVERANCE FROM THE DEVIL

When the devil entered Frank, he didn't realize the severe repercussions of what had just transpired. When a person gets possessed by a demon, he or she doesn't get to see what you see. They become a channel of the demon, unconscious of the creature within. The host also maintains control over their body most of the time, so it can be hard for them to believe your testimony when you tell them that they're a conduit of a demon. A possessed person has no memory of what just happened during an episode of possession. And even though the demon is hiding within them, it doesn't manifest itself 24/7, like some kind of monster in a zombie movie. It comes and goes, like a snake ascending from and descending into its hole. In between indisputable manifestations of demon possession, the host can still be considered, in effect, "possessed" even though they are technically highly oppressed. The difference is the degree to which the person is able to maintain some control over their body, which is a huge challenge. Demons are deceptive, and their hosts are often weak and gullible.

I used to get surprised at how those delivered from demons could be so quick to open up their lives to them again. Not anymore. However, unless you record an exorcism—which I refuse to do—they don't get to see the horror. Like a patient recovering from a surgery after hours under anesthesia, they feel different after the medical procedure, but because they were not an eyewitness to the surgery, they don't really know what just happened to them. Only the surgeons do.

One sign of possession is the inability to account for lost time or finding they have changed locations without any clue as to how they got there. With Frank, what triggered him to find help—and fast—was hearing vulgar and harassing voicemail messages his wife was receiving from a stranger. He reported them to the police. Tracing the calls, though, led back to Frank's own personal cell phone, to which he alone had access.

Strangely, many people enjoy the empowerment they feel by being inhabited by demons, even though it's wrong. Like an insecure teenager having joined a gang of bullies, it's a love-hate relationship. Frank wanted to be free from this gang, which he'd felt forced to join, but the fear of the devil's punishment made him fluctuate between seeking deliverance and then tolerating—even welcoming—the demon's return after exorcism. This obviously exacerbated the situation; as Christ explains, "the last state of that person is worse than the first" (Matt. 12:45).

After the phone calls to his wife, the demonic activity escalated, taking a terrible toll on Frank's family. A typical day would include blackouts in which Frank couldn't account for places he had been or things he had done, mostly for minutes but sometimes for hours. He would do disturbing and dangerous things. He would walk into oncoming traffic without any recollection of how he ended up in the middle of the street. He'd put on DVDs of horror movies for his kids to watch, and then scold them for watching unsuitable films.

At one point, he asked a local priest to perform a house blessing. The clergyman visited the home but left in a hurry, unwilling to give an account of what had happened but swearing never to return to the home. He was angry at Frank for hiding the fact that the house was haunted. Years later, when I tried to speak with the priest about his story, he refused. He apparently gave the family some holy water but held fast to his decision to never visit the place again.

Frank's question to me when I met him for the first time was whether I would believe what he was about to tell me. I assured him that there was very little that shocked me when it came to the sphere of the supernatural. He was relieved. Like so many victims who suffer with demonism—or whom the Bible labels as *demoniacs*—being accused of lying or dismissed as being crazy causes the greatest pain.

After he told me his story, I asked him straight-out if he wanted to be delivered from the devil. Without any hesitation, he said yes. However, what I should have done was ask him if he was prepared for the consequences. The devil's retreat from our lives always presumes a commitment to completely surrender our lives to Jesus's lordship. Otherwise, we are only using the almighty King for some temporary relief. Then after we ungrateful and myopic creatures get what we want from our good Creator, we toss the relationship aside. It's only because God is love that He puts up with this stupidity, offering us countless chances to be saved from our sinful, selfish ways.

None of us surrender ourselves very well as sinners. Any mature and humble Christian knows deep down that, daily, we break the Ten Commandments more times than we can count, as we by no means love our neighbors as ourselves.

Neither do we love God with our whole heart, mind, and soul. Yet repentance can be summarized as the sincere desire to turn from ourselves—from our sin, the world, and the devil—and toward our Lord Jesus who is filled with grace and mercy. He is our Righteousness and Savior.

Yet as Christ says, for those who aren't actually repentant, the demon "goes and brings with it seven other spirits more evil than itself, and they enter and dwell there" (12:45). Although demoniacs physically exhibit this reality, our Lord's statement has a deep spiritual application to each one of us as well. There is no room for half-hearted Christians in the Lord's army. We all need to seriously and deliberately examine our lives daily so that Jesus alone occupies the homes of our hearts, washing away every trace of evil by the forgiveness of sins He poured out upon us at the victorious cross.

I asked Frank if he would pray the Lord's Prayer with me. I do this often. This permits me a chance to monitor the degree to which the devil is physically present. After all, the zone between demonic *oppression* and *possession* is a gray one, and demonic presence involves a matter of degree. In a case of oppression, the host is partially in control of his or her body and mind, whereas with a possession, the host is a passive instrument of the demon. Although all people are tempted and attacked by the devil, demonic oppression involves the actual presence of at least one demon within someone. The entity is often "in hiding," manifesting itself to various degrees, possession obviously being the fullest. Possession is rather clear-cut. A demoniac stands before you. Oppression, on the other hand, requires a lot of discernment. It's a lot harder to address because you first need to figure out to what degree to hold the host accountable for their words and deeds. These victims have control over their lives but to a lesser degree than others. And the demonic grip can come and go in spurts.

Halfway through the Lord's Prayer, Frank stopped abruptly. Even after some prodding from me, he couldn't continue. I asked if he could speak the words "Jesus is Lord." He was unable. He was even incapable of saying "Jesus Christ." When he tried, his legs shook uncontrollably and he pounded his fists against the wall.

This came as no surprise to me. *Jesus Christ* is the holiest of names. The devil hates it and is terrified of it. When hearing it, it must feel like heaping coals on his icy skull. That is why vocalizing these powerful words in faith is essential to a successful exorcism. "At the name of Jesus every knee [shall] bow, in heaven and on earth and under the earth, and every tongue confess that Jesus Christ is Lord, to the glory of God the Father" (Phil. 2:10–11). The demons are not exempt.

At the name of Jesus, items in the room started to shake. Pictures dropped off the wall and lights began to flicker. Frank partially lost consciousness and started to physically convulse on the floor, and when he arose, he was unable to stare at me directly.

In moments like this, an exorcist must decide whether to proceed. If he chooses to stop, the host will likely "snap out of it." After all, the demon just wants to be left alone. It doesn't want to find a new residence. So it will retreat to the basement or attic of the home that it occupies, temporarily. It definitely doesn't want to meet Jesus face-to-face through His called and ordained servants.

We see this with Jesus, our Chief Exorcist, at the Gadarenes when "Legion" enters the pigs (Matt. 8:28–34) after deliverance. The demons need to go somewhere after an exorcism, even though they'd rather not. They don't like water (12:43), probably since it reminds them of holy baptism, the means

29

by which the Lord makes His home in people. And so the pigs drown, and the demons find a new victim to be their habitation.

I used to become afraid that the exorcised demon might just hop into another person nearby or, when things didn't go as planned, wonder whether I'd waited too long or had overreacted. I've found that overthinking doesn't help. There are simply too many unanswered questions to obsess over, and the devil will use every one to distract you from the mission. Although you want to take all possible precautions, trying to imagine all possible scenarios and how they can all go wrong represents a lack of trust in Christ. Instead, a maturing faith means an increased confidence in the Lord's will always being done—His good and gracious will. He's got the answers even when we don't. And it's not my business what happens to the thing afterward. My job is to react to what the Lord has just laid in my lap. And that's what I did.

Exorcizing Frank

After prayerful consideration, I decided it was time to perform an exorcism on Frank—to pull out that demonic worm. It's a delicate decision because the timing matters. On the one hand, if the individual isn't fully on board, you can make things a lot worse. Sometimes the exorcist wants deliverance more than the demoniac does; they may have mixed feelings about turning away from the devil and surrendering to Christ. On the other hand, if you wait too long, the devil just gets what he wants, such as more time to convince his host that it's a bad idea to kick him out of the house. In this case, I didn't know if I would have another chance to help Frank. Frank wanted to be free. But his commitment to the idea of the Lord taking the devil's place wasn't clear. Ideally, involving other experienced, mature Christians by seeking their advice is always the wisest and safest way to proceed.

Furthermore, when possible, I like to schedule exorcisms at churches. The devil hates the Lord's holy house, and operating in such sacred spaces is torturous to him. It's also the best choice, since pastoral ministry is an extension of the work of the wider congregation. There's no room for "Lone Ranger" Christians or pastors. Even if the pastor is alone in the sanctuary exorcising demons, it's as if the pews are filled with other believers, saints, angels, and archangels.

If an exorcist doesn't rely on Christ from start to finish, he will fail in one way or another. That's why Jesus says some demons only come out through prayer and fasting (see Matt. 17:21). Despite the popular opinion of self-righteous Christians, fasting doesn't make us strong. It doesn't function as a spiritual energy drink that gives us the extra boost needed to defeat the devil on our own. Fasting makes us weak. The physical feeling reminds us of the essential spiritual truth that we are helpless in ourselves. After all, we don't feel stronger on an empty stomach. We feel hungry. So, too, our souls are weak and famished. We have no power in ourselves. Yet "[Christ's] power is made perfect in weakness" (2 Cor. 12:9). Jesus is the "bread of life" (John 6:35). Our strength is in Jesus and is not rooted in any human abilities or personal qualities. That's why fasting and prayer are inseparable. Prayer expresses dependence on God alone. His wisdom becomes our exclusive source of help.

I commanded Frank to speak the words "Jesus is Lord" as I read passages on demon possession from the New Testament. After a few tries, like smoking out a hiding criminal squatting in someone else's building, the angry demon manifested itself with fury. It began to speak directly to me. It spoke in a language unfamiliar to the host and with an accent that was definitely not his. I happened to be fluent in the language, so I knew exactly what it was saying. Frank's whole physical demeanor changed. His face became contorted. His mannerisms were no longer his own. In a demon possession, it's as if a deformed person is trying to fit into someone else's clothing that's one size too small, or a hand with arthritis is stuffed into a tight glove. The body will often take on new characteristics or behave in unusual ways, and in some extreme cases, even do unnatural and even supernatural things. But at the very least the face changes, replacing human facial expressions with monstrous ones.

Frank was physically fit—he regularly worked out at the gym—which made me nervous. Would he beat me up? On the bright side, I was forced to rely more fully on the power of Christ. Thankfully, the demon didn't touch me. It stood only inches away, but it was as if there was an invisible hedge of holy angels protecting me from physical assault. For even when demons play tricks with the lights, noises, movements, and winds, the angels are there, silent but ready to jump in. As I stood before this demon, I felt like there was a crowd of heavenly hosts huddled around me. At the very least I could rely on my guardian angel, who could take down any demon in a heartbeat.

The Word of the Lord

When it comes to physical symptoms of demonic oppression, the first giveaway of the presence of an evil entity is the eyes. The eyes are a window to the soul. I've seen those venomous eyes enough times to get a pretty good hunch as to whether someone is oppressed. In many cases of severe oppression, sunglasses are worn by the victim. The devil hates the light—it symbolizes the spiritual reality that Christ is the

Light of the World. It's no coincidence that much crime and evil happens at night. "For you are all children of light, children of the day. We are not of the night or of the darkness" (1 Thess. 5:5). But sunglasses are also worn in the night or day to conceal the demonic presence, which can frequently be detected through human eyes. For the same reason, the oppressed often avoid people and hang their heads low. I'm obviously not suggesting that people who wear sunglasses, or those that don't stand up straight or never look you in the eye, are always a cause for alarm. These are only noteworthy signs of demonism when a slew of other symptoms are present.

Now Frank, or rather his demons (for it turned out that there was more than one), stared me in the eyes, penetrating my soul with a baleful glare. If you have never experienced this, and most people thankfully have not, it's horrific. It's even worse than hearing demons speak, though the tongue is more dangerous than the eye. Words, after all, are the most powerful weapon in the world.

In my book *My First Exorcism*, I discuss how conversing with the devil is always a bad idea. As to why I continued to fall for the trick, I don't know—may God have mercy on me. At first I rebuked and forbade Frank's demon from speaking, while commanding it to depart immediately. But then I made the mistake of saying a little more. Like Moses striking the rock without the command of God, I decided to do things my own way. I stepped out from behind Jesus, who was my wall of protection. I used my own words instead of the Lord's. I foolishly forgot that I was a steward of the Lord's gifts and people. I began operating in my own stead. I mentioned something about being familiar with the devil from a previous exorcism, a woman named Cindy who had many demons and continued to struggle with possession until her death.

The demon, intending to rattle me, which it did, grinned like the Grinch and retorted, "So how did that one go for you?" With some experience, you will notice that the devil prefers the Socratic method of asking questions so as to control the conversation. Like the serpent in the garden targeting Adam and Eve, the devil always tries to get you to doubt the truth by twisting and turning information with half-truths, a deception that will always end badly for anyone who engages in conversation with him.

The only way to resist this temptation is to say nothing and silence him (Luke 4:35), as Jesus did in the desert when He battled Satan with the Word of God (Matt. 4:1–11). For all the devil's words, whether they're voiced from the lips of a demoniac, from the letters on a tarot card, or from the mouths of false teachers, are aimed at creating doubt in hearts filled with faith.

The devil was trying to tempt me to believe that Cindy had died unsaved. I told him that his attempt to discourage me wouldn't work; though Cindy wasn't an ideal Christian and had many faults, she confessed Christ as her Savior unto her dying breath and was in heaven now. He didn't like hearing that one bit. He attempted to retreat and hide back in his host, but I wouldn't let him. I rebuked him in the mighty name of Jesus.

Frank fell onto his back, convulsing, his eyes rolled back. Then I made the mistake of engaging the demon in conversation again. I ordered it to tell me its name, in the name of Jesus. With the speed of lightning, Frank stood there directly in front of me, his distorted figure only inches from my face.

I remember being mystified by this sudden movement, the way he cut through space in a millisecond. But he stood there grinning at me with a rancorous and confident expression resembling that of the beastly Gollum from the Lord of the Rings series.

With a calm and even tone, the demon inquired, "Why do you want to know my name? You know who I am." I felt like the loser in a game of chess, when your opponent proudly pronounces the dreaded word *checkmate*, yet it takes you a few seconds to discover it for yourself. I was caught off guard and confused. It was right. I didn't need to know its name, and I definitely didn't want to get dragged down this rabbit hole of a dialogue with a creature smarter and more powerful than I. The devil is a liar, after all. To this day, I still don't understand why it asked that question. Sometimes I wonder if it was pretending to be God, the great "I Am." The fact that I still think about it means it achieved a tiny victory in my life that day. The more time we spend thinking about the devil, the less time we spend reflecting upon the Lord. That's why books like this one have their place but shouldn't become bestsellers.

Not all exorcists agree that talking with the devil is a bad idea. Some have dangerously used discussions they have had with demons to build doctrines on questions of hell, purgatory, and the distinction between ghosts and demons. I refuse to be one of those. Others have argued that you need to "cast the demon into the abyss" to prevent evil spirits from inhabiting others. I would rather leave all those matters to God's direction than speculate in ways that are displeasing in His sight.

So I proceeded by simply commanding the demon to be quiet in the name of the Triune God. I forbade it to speak at all, in the name of the Lord. This was a good call. It obeyed.

Then I pulled out all the weapons by reciting the Word of the Lord without ceasing. After I silenced it in the name of Jesus and began rebuking it with sacred phraseology, it said nothing. It just smiled and fixed Frank's eyes on mine like a statue, waiting for me to break. Frank didn't blink. He didn't move. He only breathed. That malevolent and sinister grin has left an unsettling mark on my memory ever since.

It was an intense staring contest as I spoke at it, repeating over and over again the words, "I adjure you to depart in the name of the Father, Son, and Holy Spirit," and "I rebuke you in the name of Jesus Christ, Victor and the King of the universe, your Creator." I spoke the words again and again, like a mantra, without stopping. My faith didn't waver in any of those words, though my articulation did falter whenever I became distracted by the eyes. When I did tire out, I dropped my head and closed my eyes to pray the Our Father, mumbling it softly.

It was a risky thing to do, considering Frank was twice as strong as me. I was vulnerable. It could've killed me. I kept hoping that, when I reopened my eyes, the demon would be gone. But when my head rose, there was that waxlike statue, staring and smiling.

In desperation, I pulled out my small crucifix that I had hanging around my neck. I commanded the demon to stare at that instead. It did. Immediately. Now something changed in its demeanor. Slowly the smile disappeared, and those eyes, fixated on my tiny image of Jesus suspended on the cross, became droopy and were filled with terror. The demon looked like an overconfident childhood bully getting spooked by a parent just walking into the room.

Later that day, I noticed that my crucifix, which to this day I still wear around my neck, had become dented and mangled. It's possible that my thumb and index finger squeezed the steel and golden cross so hard while I held it before the eyes of the demon that I unintentionally crushed it because of my adrenaline. But I think that's unlikely. In any case, the bottom half of it is crushed, a constant reminder to me that though Satan would strike our Lord's heel in the crucifixion, by that very act and event, He would crush his head (Gen. 3:15). Jesus did that, in a tiny way, on this day too.

The sight of the crucifix, coupled with the repetition of the divine Scriptures and Christian prayer, seemed to achieve Frank's deliverance. After thirty minutes from start to finish, I heard a *whoosh* as something fled from Frank. He fell to the ground like a stuffed toy that had just been dropped by a very active child. I was able to half catch this fainting man, who then awoke from his slumber.

He wasn't only back to normal; he was better than ever. He opened his happy eyes and gave me a real smile. A God-given, human smile. He wept. So did I. He began to praise God and thank me. And surely the angels rejoiced also, as "there is joy before the angels of God over one sinner who repents" (Luke 15:10).

As so often I find after such deliverance, not only thanks but also apologies are offered. Even though a demoniac isn't technically responsible for sins committed under demonic influence, such remorse is a natural expression of gratitude. They are sorry for the hurt that they caused. But without hurt, there is no healing. What one intends for evil, God intends for good (Gen. 50:20).

There's always a risk that there are more evil spirits residing inside the host than you first thought. They like to hide, and you don't want to leave the job unfinished. So it makes sense to ask the delivered individual whether they sense that they have been fully liberated. I asked Frank directly if he thought there was more going on inside him, but he didn't think so. Neither did I. With a little experience, you can just kind of tell.

Then Frank slept. He slept for eighteen hours straight. He stated later that he had never slept that long in his life. He rested in peace.

Embodied Souls

For many years, Frank had suffered severely with grinding his teeth. In his sleep, he would even gnash them. Grinding teeth is an obvious symptom of stress and anxiety. But gnashing teeth is also a description of hell (Matt. 13:42). Such physical signs or symptoms of spiritual occurrences shouldn't shock Christians. Whether we encounter the intersection of spirituality and physicality in positive human experiences, such as Christian worship in which believers can receive bodily healing through prayer or the sacraments, or negative ones, like in the occult and witchcraft, Christians must admit that the overlap of the spiritual and material realities of the human experience includes spiritual phenomena reflected in physical forms. After all, we aren't gnostics. Yet we are surrounded by gnostic ideas that penetrate the way we think and live.

In order to understand what was going on with Frank, and other demoniacs, and why many of us have a hard time even believing it, we Christians need to acknowledge that certain anthropological beliefs are crucial to an accurate and scriptural worldview. This is hard for us, because biblical beliefs are diametrically opposed to the world's, which are based in pagan ideas. And these false concepts influence us more than we think. Although most modern Christians have never heard of the heresy of gnosticism, its impact on the philosophical system by which the Western world is governed—and, sadly, many church bodies too—can't be overstated. When it comes to demonism, it's the reason so many Christians are rationalists and dismiss the physical displays of spiritual realities. It's also the reason Christian pastors default to mental health professionals, medicine, and pharmaceuticals when dealing with demonic manifestations in the lives of their parishioners. It's the reason books like this one are often not taken seriously.

Historically, one version of gnosticism taught that the body had no value and religion was reduced to the intellectual pursuit of pure philosophical thought. Proponents of this view thought that bodily things got in the way of spiritual progress. Other gnostics thought that their bodies and souls were essentially one and the same essence. A beautiful exterior appearance mirrored a beautiful interior spiritual state. When people live in ways that show either that they don't think their body has anything to do with their faith or that they can save their souls by the way they live, they reveal that they have drunk the Kool-Aid of gnosticism. Demon possession is a compelling argument against gnostic beliefs that support the bifurcation of body and soul.

After all, there's a correspondence between the physical world and the body and the spiritual world and the soul. Otherwise, the material world would be an ill-suited and even impossible means for the infinite God to communicate His divine gifts to finite people. The Word of God is written on paper. Physical. Jesus's body is conveyed through bread. Physical. The Holy Spirit comes through water. Physical. God uses physical means to offer His Spirit and saving grace to the physical world.

The fact that things pertaining to the spiritual sphere are joined with those of the physical sphere is quintessential to the Christian Faith.[1] Christians don't put a wedge between

---

1. The Church talks about faith in two ways: *fides qua* (personal trust, or "little-f faith") and *fides quae* (communal confession of a shared belief, or "big-F Faith").

the two spheres. If we did, we would be forced to deny the incarnation of God at Christmas and the full union into one Person of the two natures of Jesus Christ. How can God become man if the spirit can have nothing to do with flesh and blood?

Yet we live in a gnostic world buttressed by such philosophically driven demarcations, and most people live as if the body and soul have nothing in common with one another. Accordingly, the idea of evil spirits entering physical bodies doesn't jibe with their preconceived worldview.

In contrast, the Christian definition of *man*, from the Hebrew *ish*, translates to something like "embodied soul." The Creator breathed His Spirit into the dust of the ground from which man had been formed, and the man became a living being: a body and soul creature. Body and soul became one. Death is by definition the separation of body and soul. That's precisely what makes it so terrible. It's the most unnatural and appalling of human experiences. One reason that the final resurrection will be a glorious day for Christians is because the Lord will restore each redeemed person to their intended state, which includes the reuniting of their once fallen but now sanctified body and soul. After all, because the self consists of body and soul, salvation must include both.

Unsurprisingly, holy baptism is both a body and soul affair, as Jesus saves the whole sinful person through His atoning sacrificial death delivered through this sacred event. In order to save us, God had to assume our flesh through the Virgin Mary. Now He remains forever incarnate for us through the physical means of the spoken and written Word and the sacraments exemplifying the high value He places on His redeemed creation.

Yet in spite of this truth, one often hears from well-meaning Christians that the body is simply a cage for the soul, denying any real sacred union between the two. Accordingly, cremation was never part of Christian tradition. Gnostics did that. It was an attempt to free the soul from the body, as in Hinduism. Burial is the optimal way of honoring the body, proclaiming the resurrection of the dead, and confessing the belief in a glorious overlap between heaven and earth. St. Paul insists upon a physical resurrection of the body as necessary for salvation. Otherwise, "we are of all people most to be pitied" (1 Cor. 15:19). A heaven consisting of only souls and not bodies is inconceivable for Christians. As disembodied souls, we would never be complete. Humankind would never be at peace. Paradise would not be a perfectly happy place. Heaven would not be heaven. After all, when God became flesh and dwelled among us, He proved that spirituality involves physical things. Many gnostics of the New Testament time rejected the redemption of the physical world because they believed flesh and blood to be intrinsically bad. They also denied that Jesus is God.

Forms of gnosticism still permeate our society and even the Church. How many Christians deem donating their bodies to science as problematic? How many kneel for prayer? How many consult the Word of God when it comes to their sex lives? Some advocates of LGBTQ+ ideology insist that "being born the wrong gender in the wrong body" is an anthropological fact. Yet besides the idea not being grounded in science, it is underpinned by religious presuppositions and stems from ancient pagan belief systems. Everyone has faith in something. Everyone has a god. Sadly, some Christians unabashedly cherish more than one. Yet there is only one God who is Love and Truth, while all the rest are liars seeking to destroy men and women in both body and soul. They seek to separate people from God. They crave for them to suffer in hell.

The Overlap of Our Bodily and Spiritual Existences

Gnosticism takes on new forms in every generation. Because of the undeniable increase of publicity of supernatural phenomena, much of the secular world no longer denies it. They just seek scientific ways of explaining what was once labeled "the unexplained." Acts once seen as miracles are now viewed through the lens of parapsychology as scientifically possible. Hollywood movies propose clever and imaginative explanations for supernatural abilities displayed in humans. The argument is that some brains are more evolved or superior to others, harnessing the mystical powers of energy forces that surround each one of us. That's why some people can do fantastic and unbelievable things that contradict the laws of nature. ESP is considered to be a skill cultivated by those who have figured out how to tap into unexplored regions of their minds. Spiritual phenomena are reduced to physicality.

Some Christians fall into this trap. I have heard well-intentioned believers attempting to scientifically prove Christian Faith claims by arguing that the soul has weight, for example. The dead weigh less than the living. Even if this is true, it represents a perilous manner of thinking, as it seeks to rob the spiritual of its unique characteristics. It deals with the supernatural from within the humanly known sphere and seeks to interpret spiritual mysteries by means of a man-made scientistic cosmology. All this aligns well with classic gnosticism, as it attempts to reduce the spiritual realm to the material one.

Paganism of the past held that there was no sphere of reality outside this observable one. Certainly, there was an invisible realm inaccessible to mortals. But mortals and immortals both dwelled within the same bubble of a single-realm universe, governed by certain laws and operating within the parameters of time and space. For the ancient Greeks, then, the gods acted like people. They fought, drank, had sex, and killed. The human experience was their only reference for understanding how divine beings behaved. The gods had faults and were sinful. Some were stronger than others, but no single one was almighty.

Monotheism was a radical notion because it asserted that there was one God who transcended this cosmos. The gods in which the pagans believed were not gods at all. They were actually demons (1 Cor. 10:18–20).

Is it any surprise, then, that the demons seek to cast doubt on the fact that there's one almighty God who transcends the present cosmos? Instead, they pretend to be gods within a multiplicity of spiritual entities at work in our world as our friends and foes. When Indigenous peoples of North America embraced Christian missionaries, it was because Christianity made sense and was attractive. Wouldn't you rather believe in an omnipotent God of love versus a bunch of gods with limited power who, for the most part, are indifferent to your existence? The irony is that most Westerners today have gravitated back toward such pagan belief systems.

In spite of the clear, beautiful, convincing, and infallible teachings of the Holy Bible, many Christians still have difficulty believing that heavenly and earthly realities have been joined together so tightly in creation. Some ask how natural water and wine can distribute spiritual goods. The popularity of Eastern spirituality, mysticism, and meditation represents efforts at escaping the physical world as a way of tapping into the spiritual. Yet true Christianity says the opposite. We always find our Lord incarnate in very tangible ways. The man Jesus of Nazareth—God made flesh— remains hidden and yet revealed among us through physical congregations, physical sacraments, and the physical pages of a physical book. It's certainly a paradox of sorts, but God never promised that the unsearchable mysteries of the universe could be grasped by the human intellect. Instead, we are expected to believe even when we don't understand. "For who has known the mind of the Lord, or who has been his counselor?" (Rom. 11:34).

Christian worship and church services are the best examples of heavenly realities manifested in earthly ways because they take place through physical things such as the pastor and people, water and books, and bread and wine. God uses human mouths and sacred music to bless His holy name and deliver His divine gifts to us. A sermon is nothing less than God speaking on earth. Why bother singing hymns and chanting liturgies unless we believe that angels join us in an eternal song fit for the King of Kings and Lord of Lords? Do we deny these miracles because they happen amid simple wooden pews and ordinary-looking people? But just like heaven on earth is experienced by the smells, sounds, and sights of reverent, historic, and biblical worship, so, too, a twisted, corrupted, and unholy version of the supernatural is orchestrated by a devil who doesn't lack imagination. Wherever God builds a church, Satan builds a chapel.

Believing in the overlap between things pertaining to our bodily and spiritual existence is essential for a holistic approach to the ministry of deliverance. Treatments often consist of both spiritual and physical components. And as God is the Lord of both "church" and "state," pastors can find critical assistance in the medical and health care communities. But, honestly, in today's society, where physicians are viewed as demigods and medicine as the ultimate solution to all sociopsychological problems, spiritual discernment is a lot easier when helping professionals are confessing Christians.

For Frank, I was able to find a Christian psychiatrist who supported what I had begun and offered effective counseling in ways I was unable. The spiritual ministry of the apostles often included the healing of bodies alongside deliverance from the unclean spirits (Matt. 10:1; Mark 1:32–34; Luke 9:1–2; Acts 5:16). Belief in the intimate connection between the spiritual and physical dimensions of ministry resulted in some believers hoping that even the physical shadow of an apostle would land upon them (Acts 5:15). St. James instructed the Church to anoint sick bodies with oil while proclaiming the spiritual medicine of the forgiveness of sins (James 5:14–15). Some liturgical rites and prayers that employ anointing oil for bodily healing rebuke the work of the devil in the soul as well.

When Christians deny the supernatural, they demonstrate a lack of faith in God's Word and cripple their ability to minister within the demonic field. In some exorcisms, such as cases where witchcraft is the cause for possession, items such as glass, nails, knotted strings, insects, rolled wires, and even small wooden voodoo dolls are vomited out of human bodies.[2] These sights may terrify all in attendance, who are

---

2. Horrified by the unusual physical manifestation of spiritual entities, Lutheran exorcist Johann Christoph Blumhardt wrote in 1842:

> At the same time I cannot but look with the most moving gratitude upon the many preservations and deliverances which were accorded to me amid horrid scenes again and again. The patient was tortured incessantly. Her body would often swell extraordinarily, and she would vomit whole buckets of water. This seemed so strange to the doctor, who was always present, as one could not understand where all that water came from. She also received frequent blows on her head, knocks in the side, and in addition suffered from heavy nose bleeding, constipation, and other things. And with all the things going on in her, it seemed to be heading for a fatal turn. But through prayer and faith the attacks were made harmless and pushed back.

Johann Christoph Blumhardt, *Jesus Is Victor!: Blumhardt's Battle with the Powers of Darkness* (Awaken Media, 2020), 52.

likely to flee "out of that house naked and wounded" (Acts 19:16).

I remember one backslidden Christian who snuck into an exorcism in which I was involved and listened through the wall from an adjoining room. I asked him what he thought about what he'd heard behind that locked door. He argued that aliens had possessed the man, since demons didn't exist. When I asked him why the only name that delivered demoniacs from these evil entities was the holy name of Jesus, he was speechless. He scratched his head and walked away.

People will come up with all sorts of creative explanations for happenings that don't harmonize with their preconceived worldviews. I can't count the number of silly arguments I've read in academic journals and biblical commentaries arguing that the demoniacs in the biblical narratives were epileptics or psychologically disturbed. The assumption is that the ancients were just not scientifically advanced enough to know the difference. And yet, we still couldn't build the Egyptian pyramids with today's twenty-first-century technology. So much for evolution! In any case, one is hard-pressed to interpret the Holy Scriptures in such nonliteral ways. Basically, skepticism here implies that Jesus was either uninformed, superstitious, or a liar. As God enfleshed, He cannot be any of the above.

When we "advanced" moderns look around ourselves, we see nothing but what is physically here. Maybe we envision a heaven far above, but in between there and here, nothing else is present. The ancients didn't see things that way. There was no empty space for them. When they looked at the sky, they viewed themselves surrounded by a multitude of invisible hosts: saints, angels, and demons. Interacting with them through prayers, worship, and battles was just part of the normal rhythm of the day.

We need to find our way back to the ancient worldview, as we've shamefully drifted far from it by our supposedly "progressive" ways of thinking. The Bible says that angels are assigned to Christians, caring for our needs and protecting us from dangers of body and soul. A "thousand thousands" serve God, and "ten thousand times ten thousand" stand before Him (Dan. 7:10), preparing to gloriously escort our Lord at the parade of His return. We deprive ourselves of their help when we downplay their importance or even deny their existence altogether.

For the Church fathers, it was natural to think of oneself situated in the middle of a spiritual battle. They weren't gnostic but rather understood the intrinsic union of body and soul, and so physical manifestations of spiritual realities were simply assumed. It wasn't outlandish to hear stories about being rescued by an angel or assaulted by a demon. Today, if you make such claims, you'd better be a kid. Then it's cute. Otherwise, you're crazy.

Rationalist and scientific approaches to interpreting life events and making sense of the world around us are presumed by most educated people today, even though their assertions are often unsubstantiated. They "believe" in science, but when a scientific hypothesis doesn't support the doctrine of their preexisting faith, the scientific method is shoved to the side. After all, most of what we "know" to be true is acquiesced to by faith. And still, there remains so much we don't know about the universe.

Consider again empty space. Is it really empty? By no means. It's filled with particles, energy, and waves. If these things were made visible, you probably wouldn't be able to see your hand in front of your face. We have the audacity to judge the worldview of past generations whenever it doesn't align with our own. This isn't scientific. It's prejudice. But it's predictable. In a society that glorifies youth, we fail to acknowledge the biblical fact that the aged often know more than us. The Bible praises the elderly as embodying true wisdom gained through life, but we prefer to rely on ourselves for understanding. We are by nature conceited.

The ministry of deliverance is nonsense for those operating within a gnostic worldview. The premise that everything living consists only of material substance seeks answers for demonism in psychology alone. It amounts to denying the devil as real. And if you do that, you have no hope, for then he has already begun to kill you with his lies.

Kinds of Demonism

Because of the influence of pagan and gnostic worldviews, most Christians don't take the devil as seriously as they ought. Some think that if they just believe well, they will easily be saved, and they aren't concerned as to how they live. Others believe that doing their best to live a good life will get them to heaven despite neither having an orthodox faith nor attending a Bible-believing church. Yet on the one hand, giving in to bodily temptations impacts the mind and can even destroy true faith. On the other hand, the devil likes nothing more than watching "good Christians" believe they are saved by works of the flesh, so they can be distracted from saving faith in the teachings of Christ. We are all under the influence of the evil one in one way or another.

If it wasn't for the work of the Holy Spirit through the Word of Christ, we would all remain captive to the devil. The reason I say *remain* is that we were all once members of his unholy kingdom—until the Son of God rescued us through His atoning death. We were all "possessed" by the devil and have been "exorcised" by Christ.

The Church's ministry deals with two kinds of demon possession, one spiritual and one physical. We're all born "by nature children of wrath" (Eph. 2:3) and thus members of the devil's kingdom. We're all under the devil but also redeemed, "for at one time you were darkness, but now you are light in the Lord" (Eph. 5:8). We are citizens of two countries simultaneously; we are both sinners and saints.

This explains the divided allegiance we face daily, the internal wrestling between the good and evil present in every human being. Yet it's more nuanced in Christians, who have been given a new identity through faith in Christ. We are delivered by the gospel and holy baptism. The devil hates the Lord, whom he finds dwelling in us as temples of the Holy Spirit (1 Cor. 6:19). As Martin Luther once said, "When the devil harasses us, then we know ourselves to be in good shape! The worst temptation is no temptation."[3]

So we shouldn't be surprised by the emotionally taxing spiritual civil war inside ourselves we endure as the sinner-saints we are: "For I do not understand my own actions. For I do not do what I want, but I do the very thing I hate" (Rom. 7:15). We all need ongoing deliverance here. God does it by His constant healing and forgiveness offered in His holy Word and sacraments. Yet there's a huge distinction between an ordinary, spiritual type of demonic presence in the life of a Christian who, though a saint, remains a sinner for the duration of his or her life, and the extraordinary type encountered by someone under Satan's physical influence. The tools we use in battling the second kind—the controversial of the two—require some detailed explanation.

3. As quoted in Gordon Rupp, *The Righteousness of God: Luther Studies* (Hodder & Stoughton, 1964), 115.

Although all of us struggle with demonic temptation and spiritual onslaughts, we don't all suffer from devilish attacks manifested in physical symptoms. Sometimes the differences are obvious, and sometimes they are subtle. I offer some humble guidelines to help you discern the difference.

Before conversion, all people remain spiritually possessed by the devil. The devil has taken their souls captive. If they die in a state of unbelief, they'll be taken by the devil to hell. But the devil doesn't usually control their bodies. They aren't puppets. People make rational decisions about how to live, what to eat, where to work, who to see. They are possessed *spiritually* but still free in many regards. They are not *physically* possessed.

The Church's solution to this kind of "demon possession" is an exorcism through baptism and ongoing spiritual defense through Christian ministry: studying Scripture, hearing sermons, and digesting the Word of God in various other ways in godly worship. Christians don't go to Church primarily to give God something. God doesn't need anything. We go to receive the gifts, power, and strength of the Lord. Through biblically based and Christ-centered Christian worship, Jesus battles for us, equipping us with indispensable spiritual armor.

Even though it looks as if nothing special is going on while we're sitting in a church among a motley crew of strangers— some elderly, others weak, some odd—the demonic battle is intense. Pastors feel exhausted after leading services not because they gave a speech, served a meal, and read a text for a religious ceremony. Rather, they have engaged in active spiritual warfare, which takes a toll on the body as well as the soul. There's a clear connection between the exorcism of demons and the proclamation and preaching of God's Word in the ministry of Jesus (Mark 1:39; 3:14; 6:12–13). Every

Christian service delivers repentant sinners from demons through the confession and absolution of sins, the proclamation of God's law and gospel, creedal declarations of the common Faith, intercession through the name of Jesus, and the reception of Holy Communion.

Again, the first type of demonic possession is spiritual. Yet before we discuss the second type—physical—we need to explore the nature and intent of demons: what they are and what they're up to.

3

WHAT ARE DEMONS?

Who is the devil, and what are demons?

The Bible tells us that demons are fallen angels and the devil is their leader (Luke 11:15; Rev. 12:9). One-third of the angels rebelled against God at some point after their creation and were hurled out of heaven (Rev. 12:4). They didn't want to have fellowship with their good and loving God, so He delivered them up to the freedom they sought.

Like the first humans in the garden of Eden, these arrogant angels rejected their status as *creatures* and sought to usurp the position of their *Creator*, becoming their own "gods." They're rightly referred to as *false gods* in the Bible (Deut. 32:16–17) as they create nothing. They're unable. Even when they do supernatural things, they use someone else's goods: God-created matter. Only God can perform true miracles. There's only one Creator upon whom all creation depends. Like all creatures, even those that hate God, demons are still 100 percent reliant upon God for whatever life they still possess, even though they are prisoners of hell.

Satan's ability to "create" is limited to abusing that which almighty God has created. After all, what is evil other than the absence of good? Evil can only be defined in negative terms. You can only talk about what it isn't, such as how it's different from good. Consider how darkness isn't a thing in itself but rather the absence of something: light. You can't define darkness without referencing light, whereas you can define light without mentioning darkness. For example, light can be defined as a particle and a wave with certain qualities, while darkness can only be talked about in terms of a lack of light's characteristics. All that to say: Lucifer has no creative energies in himself. The things he does and says are corruptions and abuses of things and words God has done and said. He owns nothing and creates nothing. The Creator has no competitors. The devil pretends to own things but is actually only a lying thief. When it comes to "demon possession" he doesn't rightfully "possess" anything.

Truth as Our Main Weapon of Spiritual Warfare

During my first exorcism, the devil whispered through the mouth of a young, violent, and suicidal girl the eerie words, "She's mine." I was paralyzed with fear—until I stopped believing his lie. Yet if I'd based my judgment on appearances instead of God's Word, the claim would have been pretty convincing. That's why a main strategy in the ministry of deliverance is truth-telling: convincing the victim that they belong to Jesus, who is Lord of all (Acts 2:36). And those who are terror-stricken of the devil's revenge upon those who reject him need to be reminded that God remains King over not only His loyal subjects but also the rebellious ones: "In his hand are the depths of the earth; the heights of the mountains are his also" (Ps. 95:4).

The exorcist may even need to remind the demon that it cannot have this precious creature of God. Instead, it's being evicted since it is a trespasser and impostor. The same principle applies to objects such as houses that contain evil spirits. The evil entity owns nothing. But the devil is a brilliant liar. He's a master at persuading people that he's in control by the spectacles he performs inside their homes. Incidentally, this is why the Word, which is truth, is the Christian's main weapon for offensive and defensive warfare: It chases the devil away and provides protection from his lies.

Because the Word of God is truth, and faith comes by hearing this Word (Rom. 10:17), the worst offense to God doesn't concern how we live but rather what we believe. Bad works follow a bad faith. The first sin in the garden of Eden wasn't eating the forbidden fruit and disobeying God's command. It was lack of faith. Adam and Eve mistrusted God's holy Word.

The devil asks, "Did God really say?" (Gen. 3:1 NIV), and we question. After Adam and Eve doubted, they acted in an evil way. Just as good fruit is produced by true faith, bad works stem from false faith. And faith has everything to do with its object: in what or in whom it believes. True doctrine matters. "If anyone comes to you and does not bring this teaching, do not receive him into your house or give him any greeting, for whoever greets him takes part in his wicked works" (2 John 10–11).

True teaching about God, and about how we are saved from our sinful state and broken relationship with Him, is at the heart of Christianity and salvation. There's no such thing as "subjective truth." This is a devilish lie. There's only truth, and it's always objective.

Instead of privileging true teaching and actively denouncing false teaching (Titus 1:11), *diversity* is the catchword today. This includes matters of religious beliefs. "How dare you judge another religion as false! Who do you think you are, God?"

Well, not God, but the judgments of the Church are grounded in His holy, inspired Word. The world sees no real value in traditional religion as either a help, when it comes to true religion, or a threat, when it comes to false religion. Instead, people create their own belief systems, identities, and purposes. These are all religious, too, whether one admits it or not. The word *create* is crucial here. We all find ways to reject our status as a creature and seek to become the Creator. We yearn to live by our own rules, which means no real rules.

This was the chief error of the demons. Like Adam and Eve in their first sin, we don't want to let God be God but rather want to take His place. We want to be God. We want to worship however we wish, decide our sexual identity, assert our supposed right over our bodies, and make the Holy Bible harmonize with our twisted and secularized values and immorality. In this manner, we follow in the footsteps of the devil and the fallen angels who revolted before us.

All this sin is a perversion of the good. And all perversion is demonic. It all amounts to rejecting one's place before God as creature and not letting Him be the Creator that He is. Now, God graciously reunites Himself to us, His rebellious children, becoming our Father through faith and baptism. That's why Jesus died on the cross and rose from the grave. But there's no denying that, though redeemed by the blood of Christ, Christians remain sinners. Every day we behave as rebellious and perverted children in breaking the law of God. We all practice innovative and unholy ways of failing to love God or our neighbors as ourselves in thought, word, and deed. The good news is that God still considers us His.

"For in Christ Jesus you are all sons of God, through faith" (Gal. 3:26).

The difference between believers and unbelievers isn't that we're less sinful but that we confess our sins, repent, and are forgiven. Non-Christians have inadvertently opened the door of their hearts, souls, and lives to the evil one and his hordes. St. Peter was as guilty as Judas. Peter denied Jesus three times. One could even argue that Judas was more remorseful, leading him to utter despair. The difference between the two wasn't the degree of their sinfulness but the presence or absence of faith: The apostle Peter believed in Jesus as the Son of God and trusted in His unfailing mercy. Judas didn't.

One Lord, One Faith, One Religion

One blessing I've seen in serving immigrant populations from the developing world to North America is that it can offer Christians a chance to evangelize communities we might not otherwise be able to reach. While serving as a pastor in an ethnically diverse neighborhood, I witnessed how the Holy Spirit was faithfully at work finding creative ways of spreading the gospel among Muslim refugees. In their countries of origin, the preaching of the gospel was illegal. So God brought them to the West, which offered us a unique ministry opportunity. I found them to be much hungrier for God's Word than their neighbors who had been raised in the West. I couldn't keep up with their demand for the Word. I can't count the number of women who hid scriptural tracts in their burkas or men who took ESL classes as an excuse to come to Bible study.

However, multiculturalism can also pose a spiritual threat. The most pagan and confused churches in the New Testament were those exposed to false religion, like the Corinthians. In the Old Testament, the decline of the short-lived glory of Israel under King Solomon was mostly attributed to his tolerance of false gods for the sake of his pagan wives. Celebrating false religions and preferring your cultural roots before your faith in Christ is idolatrous. The doctrinal culture of the Holy Christian and Apostolic Church (as we confess in the Apostles' Creed) needs to trump all other affiliations.

Christians need to be clear. Culture isn't neutral. Celebrating multiculturalism, when it involves embracing different religious belief systems that are untrue, is harmful to the true Faith. When peoples worshiped with totem poles, they did it because they feared the punishment of the animistic gods. Others who ceremonially drank the blood of beasts believed it helped strengthen them in warfare against their enemies. Human sacrifices among the ancients were intended to appease the wrath of the gods. Christianity offered a refreshing alternative, which is one reason it became the most popular religion in the world, spreading to every corner of the globe. Today, most of the best elements of Western civilization can be attributed to Christianity.

Christians have always confessed that their religion was the only true one. When the book of Revelation describes the population of heaven as "a great multitude that no one could count, from every nation, tribe, people and language, standing before the throne and before the Lamb" (7:9 NIV), it isn't saying that the religious cultures of all peoples are represented in heaven. Rather, it praises the fact that faith in Jesus Christ surpasses all cultural and linguistic differences.

All believers are made one in Christ *in spite* of their cultures, not *because* of them. God made different ethnicities but not cultures. Those were largely a result of humanity's sinful rebellion at Babel. In other words, God isn't prejudiced, racist, or discriminatory. He loves all people equally, which is why He rejects all religious ideas that contradict the one truth. Where God unites, the devil divides, and vice versa. Here, the devil seeks to unite cultures under the auspice that all religions provide access to the same divinity in their own unique ways. *Syncretism* is the mixing of religions into an ungodly hybrid. Sadly, most denominations do this to various degrees. They inadvertently manufacture new false religions.

Some American churches, for example, have imported smudging ceremonies in their services as an effort to welcome Native Americans, in hopes that they will start coming to church. Though well intended, such missiological tactics cheapen grace and compromise faith. The Word of God that is Truth converts all without aid. "You did not choose me, but I chose you" (John 15:16).

We don't need to sugarcoat the gospel or devise clever ways of making it more palatable to other cultural contexts. Our Triune God is cross-cultural. He loves all people. *He* will find a way and asks us only to believe Him. By faithfully teaching the truth, we help to fulfill His will of loving all people.

Jesus was Jewish but He was *the* Man for all people. On the cross He represented all humankind, without any distinctions, before the judgment seat of God. "The first man was from the earth, a man of dust; the second man is from heaven" (1 Cor. 15:47). Those who trust in Him alone as Savior are now *in* Him. Accordingly, "Just as we have borne the image of the man of dust, we shall also bear the image of the man of heaven" (v. 49).

But instead of emphasizing the places where all people groups are unified in our Lord Jesus Christ, early Jesuit missionaries looked for unity in many of the wrong places. They trivialized biblical doctrines that they thought were not essential to salvation. They permitted false teachings and practices because they wanted to respect cultural norms and find clever ways of presenting Jesus in various cultural contexts.

Today, Roman Catholicism in Mexico still includes images of demons in local churches. These inclusivist missionary efforts, minimizing the differences in religious doctrines, largely failed. If the Old Testament is a guideline, God isn't okay with sharing His throne with false gods. "For they provoked him to anger with their high places; they moved him to jealousy with their idols" (Ps. 78:58). God is jealous because He is Love.

Inasmuch as any true shepherd doesn't want to share his or her sheep with a hireling who cares about the money and not the lambs, our Lord is committed to our welfare. He alone is the Good Shepherd who willingly lays down His life for the sheep, even offering that life to the wolves on our behalf (John 10:11–18). In short, He loves us too much to share us with the devil.

Historically, overseas mission work centered on teaching and preaching that Jesus Christ is the Savior from sin, death, hell, and the devil. But now it seems it has become mainly an investment in humanitarian projects. What changed? In spite of the inescapable themes of sin and the devil in the Scriptures, hymns, collects, liturgies, and prayers of the Church, many Christians no longer believe in hell but assert that all are saved, and thus no longer see a need for missions. The idea is, if everyone can be saved through their own religions, Christian missionaries are a waste of time and money. Because of the glorification of multiculturalism and belief in the equal value of all religions, most Christians are afraid of appearing imperialistic. Real missions are considered colonialist, so we shy away from bold efforts to share the gospel outside of our nations.

But Christianity makes no sense without reference to evil and hell. From what, then, did Christ rescue us? Many people today don't like the thought that they're sinners in need of a savior. They're offended by the notion that their spiritual lives are endangered by real demons.

Christianity has always been controversial, since religious truth is rarely popular. Truth is never determined by a democratic vote. True Christians are a minority. Still, the Church remains a mighty citadel, fortified by Christ and His holy angels. And in this army, every Christian has an important role to play. Each one, a warrior for the truth, is also a suffering martyr.

If the Great Commission still applies today, which it does, the devil will do all he can to hinder the mission as he targets the best of the Lord's spiritual soldiers: confessors and defenders of the Christian Faith who stand up for the truth "in season and out of season" (2 Tim. 4:2).

The world is in a state of spiritual confusion. And that, in brief, is the nature of the demonic. One of the most important Church fathers in Christian history, St. Augustine, in *The City of God*, describes how a demon is ultimately a creature that is confused about its identity.[1] Angels are tools and agents of God. Demons reject that instrumentality, leading to confusion within themselves and their divinely ordained purposes—an eternal exasperation into which they love to recruit us by abusing not only sex, religion, and medicine (drugs) but all God's good gifts.

Just consider the unprecedented popularity of pointed attacks on the two sexes and the deplorable confusion this has caused among children and young people. The devil hates

---

1. St. Augustine of Hippo, *The City of God*, vol. 1, trans. Marcus Dods (T&T Clark, 1913), 81.

the orders of creation. God made man and woman beautiful, and so the devil is determined to mix up gender roles in such absurd and outlandish ways. But it's no joke. Suicide rates among youth are escalating, partially driven by existential questions of identity.[2]

The first thing every Christian needs to know about spiritual warfare and demonism is that the devil hates order and is the author of confusion. A heightened awareness of his tactics can minimize his ability to invade you and those around you, as well as equipping you to deal with him when he does.

Definition of Demon

Demons are all about *confusion*—abusing God's good gifts to twisted ends. This includes abusing their own confused identity. Demons don't want to *be* what they *are*. Loathing their status as servants, they reject their place in the cosmological hierarchy (Jude 6). Our Lord warns, "When you see the abomination of desolation standing where he ought not to be (let the reader understand), then let those who are in Judea flee to the mountains" (Mark 13:14).

Unlike their angelic counterparts, demons refuse to remain God's messengers and helpers, taking residence in places to which they're not assigned. Because they reject their identity as servants, and wish to seize the place of the King, they abhor being *used* and lust to exist as *ends*, even though that unique position is already filled by God Himself, who is the

2. See, for example, American Foundation for Suicide Prevention, "Suicide Statistics," accessed December 18, 2024, https://afsp.org/suicide-statistics/; CDC Suicide Prevention, "Suicide Data and Statistics," accessed December 18, 2024, https://www.cdc.gov/suicide/facts/data.html; Rachel Dowd, "More Than 40% of Transgender Adults in the US Have Attempted Suicide," UCLA School of Law: Williams Institute, July 20, 2023, https://williamsinstitute.law.ucla.edu/press/transpop-suicide-press-release/.

single *end* of all things. The Lord is the sole source of peace, rest, love, and joy, although demons adamantly deny it. Accordingly, every creature's fulfillment is distinctly in Him.

True peace and rest for the Christian are found only in God because, at the end of the day, we have a single use. Just as a light bulb finds satisfaction solely in a light socket, having no other use, so worship is the manner in which human beings are plugged into God, our sole source of eternal contentment. Is it any surprise, then, that demons are counterfeit lights (2 Cor. 11:14), posing as saviors and helpers and sources of truth, knowledge, and wisdom?

But due to our sinful and corrupt nature, we have allied ourselves with the devil, a false, inadequate socket and empty void. He is the begetter of death, robber of life, root of all evil and vice, instigator of envy, font of avarice, fomenter of discord, and author of all pain and sorrow.

We are clueless to the fact that our simple dissatisfactions betray our true allegiance. Yet just like the demons, *we* don't want to be what we *are*. We reject *our* instrumentality. Notwithstanding our identity as children of light, we are all too easily attracted to the shadows and the darkness. The rhetoric of human servanthood rings inherently offensive, suggesting images of oppression by eighteenth-century slave drivers mistreating enslaved persons.

Scorn of one's true identity and spurn of one's place and role in God's order are characteristic of the demonic. Accordingly, they are riotous monsters of chaos. In the Eastern Church, sin isn't described in terms of a deliberate, willful opposition to God. Instead, the sinful nature is framed within a discourse of humankind's inability to know ourselves and God clearly: a confusion of identity. Because of this disconnect with their true being, demons and unbelievers are never at rest and will never enjoy true community.

During one exorcism, a demon was quoted describing hell in the following way:

> Everyone lives folded within himself and torn apart by his regrets. There is no relationship with anyone; everyone finds himself in the most profound solitude and desperately weeps for the evil that he has committed.[3]

For creatures that find their satisfaction, fulfillment, and peace in something that lies outside of their own person-hood, hell is the ultimate expression of navel-gazing, as creatures abide in a pathetic yet avoidable state of uselessness for all eternity.

The demonic, then, always involves the idea of lack of order and, therefore, confusion. Their followers are residents of Babylon, translated from the Hebrew as *confusion*. Demons hate their place in the divine order of things as servants and will live in a state of dissatisfaction—forever. After turning away from their Lord and Maker in rebellion, "there was no longer any place for them in heaven" (Rev. 12:8). By denying their God-given role and purpose, they live in a restless state of confusion.[4] Therefore, according to St. Augustine, they never enjoy peace.[5] To put things very mildly, they're like spoiled, bratty children who don't get their way and throw a tantrum. Out of spite and jealousy, they want to include as many other creatures as they can find to join in their frenzy—including us. Like vandals aim only to harm, achieving no benefit for themselves, the devil just wants to injure his Lord and Creator by getting at Him at His soft spot: love.

---

3. Gabriele Amorth, *An Exorcist Tells His Story* (Ignatius Press, 1999), 76.
4. Augustine, *City of God*, 66–69.
5. Augustine, *City of God*, 318, 378.

This is why the temptations of Jesus were tempting to Jesus. They struck to the heart: His love for humankind. "Turn stones into bread so that you can care for the poor. Toss yourself off the roof of the temple so sinners will believe and be saved." Jesus's rebuke of Peter, "Get behind me, Satan!" (Matt. 16:23), was driven by His relentless devotion to die for humankind on the cross. Jesus may well have preferred to keep hanging out with His friends, feeding the hungry, and doing miracles on earth. But love compelled Him to sacrifice His human will to His divine.

Although the demons are no match for our Lord, they remain devoted to pulling the rest of God's creation into their self-created misery. They are rabidly consumed with a lust for spreading their rebellion among people. Their evil attitudes, perversions, and sentiments are contagious. They want us to reject our role and purpose as servants of the one true God and to find meaning elsewhere. They want us to live our lives in confusion, for all eternity.

Deceivers

In achieving that goal, you may be surprised to hear that the devil doesn't usually want to paralyze us with fear. Deceiving us is a more effective strategy. People won't die for the things they fear, but they'll die for their convictions. This is one reason why demon possessions are rare. They frighten people into faith.

I know several converts who came to believe that Christianity was the true religion by witnessing delivery from demons through the holy name of Jesus. Haunted houses and poltergeists have chased many people back to church. So for the most part, the devil chooses to appear as an "angel of light" (2 Cor. 11:14). His subtle tactics are far more effective in influencing the ways in which we view the world and derive meaning from our experiences.

The Word of God challenges us "not to be outwitted by Satan" by being "ignorant of his designs" (2:11). Flung headlong from the heights of heaven, the devil prowls around like a lion "going to and fro on the earth, and . . . walking up and down on it" (Job 2:2). Be careful not to doubt his abilities just because you don't see him hard at work in supernatural ways, because his strategies are not obvious. If they were, you would pray more and fast more, which is what he doesn't want to happen!

Obviously, if the evil foe appeared clothed in all his natural ugliness, he would scare us away. Instead, he wants to attract us. The devil prefers sheep's clothing to a terrifying monster costume. But beauty is a great deceiver.

Master of Disguises

Protecting ourselves from the assaults of the devil involves familiarizing ourselves with his disguises. This doesn't entail obsessing over them. Too many Christians are fooled into thinking about the devil so much that their thoughts are deflected from glorifying God. Instead, "set your minds on things that are above, not on things that are on earth. For you have died, and your life is hidden with Christ in God" (Col. 3:2–3).

But let's not be ignorant of evil designs either. We have heard how Lucifer disguises himself as an angel of light. When it comes to their relationship with humankind, the good angels' main purpose is firstly to be *heralds* or *messengers*. Secondly, angels are helpers God sends to protect us from evil. So let's consider how these two jobs get corrupted by Satan. His "angelic service" is now twisted. He is a false messenger and false helper, as well as a liar and murderer (John 8:44).

The best service angels offer human beings is communicating the Word of God to us. We find this throughout the Holy Scriptures as angels are used by God as His holy messengers. Announcing the birth and the resurrection of our Lord and Savior are the most prominent and familiar examples.

Now that the Bible has been completed and canonized, this role of angels is no more. There are no new messages from heaven (Rev. 22:18). "But even if we or an angel from heaven should preach to you a gospel contrary to the one we preached to you, let him be accursed" (Gal. 1:8). Yet unsurprisingly, the devil and his minions, as false messengers, continue to deceive the world through new words which are necessarily false words expounding false doctrines: "For false christs and false prophets will arise and perform great signs and wonders, so as to lead astray, if possible, even the elect" (Matt. 24:24).

All false teachings, whether we find them within Christianity or in other world religions, bring serious destruction to the human soul (2 Pet. 2:2). False doctrine tells lies about who humans are, who God is, and how we are saved. These lies deceive us into either self-righteousness or despair, leading us to believe that we are able to save ourselves or that we have no hope. Notice when St. Paul trains the Corinthians in spiritual warfare, equipping them with the armor of God, he frames the battle as one primarily against false teaching like non-Christian "thoughts," theological "arguments," and worldly perspectives or "lofty opinions":

> For though we walk in the flesh, we are not waging war according to the flesh. For the weapons of our warfare are not

of the flesh but have divine power to destroy strongholds. We destroy arguments and every lofty opinion raised against the knowledge of God, and take every thought captive to obey Christ. (2 Cor. 10:3–5)

Murderers and Liars

Is it any wonder, then, that the demons' greatest strategy against us is lying? False doctrine expresses ideas such as: "You are worthless. You have no purpose. Life is meaningless. Jesus didn't die for you." When I was a military chaplain, the majority of my suicide interventions involved convincing the depressed and despairing of the simple truth that God loved them.

One demonically oppressed man wouldn't stop shaking his head in angry denial while vehemently slapping himself in the face as I repeatedly told him that Jesus had forgiven him all his sins. After being subjected to that message for several minutes, he finally broke down in tears, praising Jesus for His love.

I can't count the number of times demonically oppressed people, after being freed from their bondage, have confessed to having heard such lying voices in their heads, which often follow up with, "Stay away from the pastor!" Praise the Lord that the Holy Spirit got involved!

One woman I knew escaped from a mental institution as she followed the directives of these voices, which also tempted her to kill herself. God intervened and saved her from herself. Even if it's psychological, it's always spiritual too. The voices, feelings, temptations, and intuitions are clearly demonic.

Other false voices echo diabolical teachings embedded in your conscience that want to build you up in yourself:

"You don't need Jesus. You're a good person. You can get to heaven fine on your own." Words are powerful. After all, "the word of God is living and active, sharper than any two-edged sword, piercing to the division of soul and of spirit, of joints and of marrow, and discerning the thoughts and intentions of the heart" (Heb. 4:12).

Yet false words also have dangerous effects on souls. The old saying "Sticks and stones may break my bones, but words will never hurt me" doesn't hold true. The most persuasive lies contain some truth. The absence of the full truth makes them deadly. Those tempted to suicide may have just cause for their feelings. So the evil one likes to keep them uninformed of the full story—that they have hope in God and the gospel—so that he can carry out his murderous plan.

Consider the first sin, when Adam and Eve were tempted to doubt God's word. The devil told them they could become like God. To some extent, the statement was true. Adam and Eve *would* know the difference between good and evil—something that only God knew—if they disobeyed God and ate the fruit of the Tree of Knowledge. But the way they would know it would be very different. They, not intrinsically but effectively, *became* evil, through their corrupted wills, hearts, and desires. Whereas before they only knew good, since they were only good, now they intimately knew evil. They got a lot more than they bargained for!

The devil is rightly characterized as the liar who deceives the whole world (Rev. 12:9). His strongest muscle against us is his tongue. And what a masterful and devious muscle that is, even to the point of causing suicide to innumerable despairing hearts. After all, the devil was a murderer from the beginning as there is no truth in him. When he lies, he speaks out of his own character, for he is a liar and the father of lies (John 8:44).

The demonically oppressed aren't usually ready to admit that they're under the influence of the devil. Telling them the truth about what you think about the matter, without softening it or watering it down, is critical to this ministry. The temptation is to offer every other explanation or excuse for bad behavior before stating the obvious. Most Christians these days don't want to level with others when it comes to sin. It's not politically correct to judge. But asserting truths such as, "You're going to hell unless you repent and turn to Jesus," is key to helping create the circumstances to set the person free. Instead of referring people to the doctor, telling a suspected demonically oppressed acquaintance that their issue isn't normal and honestly sharing your spiritual concerns is the Christian thing to do. Yes, it's awkward. Yes, it takes courage. But remember: You are not being mean or insensitive. You're showing love.

Judas believed that there was no forgiveness for him. He confessed his crime of betraying an innocent man but was led by Satan to believe that suicide was the only way out. So here we see what a false helper the devil is.

Lies Are the Devil's Chief Weapon

Many people are attracted to Eastern religions and seek the assistance of spirit guides to coach them through life. Some tolerate an evil spirit in their home, even arguing that it's the soul of a beloved ancestor.

One woman was very happy to welcome the alleged spirit of an Indigenous child in her bedroom after finding out the home was built on an ancient burial site. After a house blessing that declared the dwelling place as the Holy Spirit's, not to be shared with the devil, the phantom never returned. Don't be fooled: There's no such thing as a friendly ghost.

When it comes to the devil, fear, suffering, and death are always the goal. He is a murderer, and lies are his chief weapon.

His lies, then, are most effective and pernicious when it comes to assessing our value before God and the saving grace of God through the forgiveness of sins. Although we all deserve eternal death and hell, God has offered us salvation through Jesus Christ: "For by grace you have been saved through faith. And this is not your own doing; it is the gift of God, not a result of works, so that no one may boast" (Eph. 2:8–9).

Since the ascension of Christ, the devil's main manner of attack has been to deprive people of that truth so he can drag more to hell with him. After all, hell wasn't created for humanity but for him (Matt. 25:41).

The Presence and Absence of God

But creatures are created to live forever, and demons by virtue of being angels and humans by virtue of having souls need a place to spend eternity. So where else can demons dwell if they're barred from heaven? Or better stated, they have chosen to distance themselves from the kingdom of God. If heaven is characterized by abiding in the presence of our good and holy God, hell is existing in the absence of God, apart from Him. Even unbelievers enjoy the immense and wonderful gifts of God in life. They enjoy good food, caring relationships, happy feelings, and beautiful sights, smells, and sounds. Once they die, they are deprived of all these good things. Since it all comes from God, there is none of that in hell.

In a sense, hell is the ultimate freedom: freedom from God and His holy community of saints and angels. But that doesn't by any means make it good. To the contrary.

It makes it hell. For all creatures are to find their life solely in the one true God, maker of heaven and earth, for "in him we live and move and have our being" (Acts 17:28), which is why all creation "waits with eager longing for the revealing of the sons of God" (Rom. 8:19). Freedom from God is hell. And it's a hell that unbelievers already experience on earth by their lack of a relationship with the living God.

As a matter of fact, every time Christians attend church, they enter into the heavenly realms, as God meets people on earth through His Word and sacraments. The book of Revelation depicts this mystery, couched in symbolic images and language. But the idea is clear: In Christian worship we meet God. Why else does the devil seek ways to mock it with occult rituals such as the black mass, to the point of Satanists even stealing consecrated bread and wine from Christian sanctuaries?

Satanic worship turns true worship upside down in an attempt to make a foolery of the truth. There's good reason why unbelievers avoid divine worship and feel uncomfortable hearing the Bible. They wouldn't feel comfortable in heaven either, nor would they enjoy worshiping the God they rejected or despised on earth. Yet that doesn't make hell a better place for them. It just makes it more suitable.

A light bulb remaining outside of the socket for which it was crafted is forever unfulfilled and frustrated in a state of unrest. It never bears the light it was intended to shine as it fails to find its resting place, disconnected from its power source. The satanic idea that the party is in hell is just a deceitful trick to tempt people to go there. But those gullible enough to believe it are in for a big surprise.

Satan's argument in Milton's *Paradise Lost* that it is "better to reign in hell than to serve in heaven" is deluded. It fails to acknowledge that the greatest human freedom is to be a servant to God, who is our liberator. Just as He created the world for our first human ancestors, He has created heaven for our joy. In fact, this King proves it by becoming our servant. "For even the Son of Man came not to be served but to serve, and to give his life as a ransom for many" (Mark 10:45).

Adversary and Accuser: A Divine Tool

The devil seeks to deprive and distract the world from the Lord's salvation. The devil's obsession with suicide and murder is a practical one: He can get his victims to hell quicker, allowing less time for them to repent, turn to their Savior (and his archenemy) Jesus, and be saved.

Consider abortion, which occurs to at least seventy-six million children annually according to the WHO, representing the worst conceivable genocide in the history of the world.[6] The devil wants to halt the birth of these precious little creatures, and, moreover, stop their rebirth through baptism, a devious effort to depopulate the elect of heaven.

God says, "Go and multiply," and the devil finds various creative ways to hinder that from happening. Yet countless guilt-ridden parents, many of whom experience haunting, devilish, phantom crying of babies after choosing to terminate the lives of their offspring, eventually find themselves at the foot of Christ's cross to find forgiveness, life, and hope. "And we know that for those who love God all things work together for good, for those who are called according to his purpose" (Rom. 8:28). Honest and humble confession

---

6. World Health Organization, "Abortion," May 17, 2024, https://www.who.int/news-room/fact-sheets/detail/abortion.

remains the door to our Lord's forgiveness and presence. The devil knows this, so he gets to work keeping us wallowing in our sin and self-pity.

Accordingly, in an effort to entice us to join him in hell, Satan's best strategy is as our adversary (1 Pet. 5:8), which is what his name means. He's an expert in matters of justice and human weakness: "Then Satan answered the LORD and said, 'Skin for skin! All that a man has he will give for his life'" (Job 2:4). He's a skilled accuser of God's people, reminding them of their sins and unworthiness before God:

> And I heard a loud voice in heaven, saying, "Now the salvation and the power and the kingdom of our God and the authority of his Christ have come, for the accuser of our brothers has been thrown down, who accuses them day and night before our God." (Rev. 12:10)

Through accusations that we are worthless, unredeemable sinners, he enslaves us by guilt, shame, and the fear of death (Heb. 2:14–15). *Devil* literally means "slanderer." Slanderers throw accusations at us in order to poison the truth with half-truths. They seek to ruin our reputation or have us doubt our Christian identity. The devil maliciously throws our sins at us to haunt us and overbear us. "Then he showed me Joshua the high priest standing before the angel of the LORD, and Satan standing at his right hand to accuse him" (Zech. 3:1). To prevent us from being liberated from the bondage of our sins, he keeps us away from Christ-centered and biblically sound churches. He incites us to question and avoid the holy Word of God. But going to church or reading the Bible will only get you so far, unless you have a living faith. Even in the case of demonically oppressed Christians, you may find them attending worship and even participating.

It's all part of demonic deception, duping fellow Christians into thinking it's not as bad as it is. Even Judas, "a devil" (John 6:70), walked with Jesus, yet not for the right reasons.

But believe it or not, even here there's good news. What is fascinating and comforting is that God still uses this wicked serpent for His good and divine purposes, whether the devil likes it or not. For though he knows nothing about God's grace, Jesus does. And the evil adversary's accusations unintentionally prepare people for the One who takes the punishment we deserve for our sins upon Himself. Just as the malicious high priest, Caiaphas, was a crucial instrument of God in the crucifixion of our Lord—even prophetically, since "it was Caiaphas who had advised the Jews that it would be expedient that one man should die for the people" (John 18:14)—God uses the devil for good.

4

HOW TO DEAL
WITH THE DEVIL

When dealing with the devil, we need first to fully understand and firmly believe that we have the upper hand. Satan is an instrument of God, even though that fact must be more torturous to his gang of thugs than swimming in the hottest pool of lava. Pretending that he's free and independent changes nothing. Consider how God used Joseph's brothers and their evil plan when they sold Joseph into slavery "to bring it about that many people should be kept alive, as they are today" (Gen. 50:20). The devil remains a divine tool of God that serves His glorious purposes. In fact, the devil cannot act without God's permission, as we see with his tempting of Job. Is it surprising, then, that the plans of the devil always backfire? Even when it appears that the devil is victorious, it's simply never true.

Consider how the devil's accusations against us often drive us to Christ. He certainly is skilled at accusing us of our sin and making us feel rightfully guilty. When we think we are righteous in ourselves, beautiful in the sight of God on our own merits, the accuser is an effective teacher and even preacher of the law as he shows us how spiritually ugly we actually are. When we carefully gaze into the mirror of the Ten Commandments, we see how horrendously we break them throughout the day. Our Lord uses the devil to bring us to that recognition, so that the Holy Spirit can take over and lead us to the righteousness of Christ Jesus. In Him we have complete spiritual beauty. In this sense, "the greatest temptation is to have no temptation" as St. Bernard of Clairvaux supposedly said. The demands of Scripture "imprisoned everything under sin, so that the promise by faith in Jesus Christ might be given to those who believe" (Gal. 3:22).

Once convicted of sin by the hearing of the law, we can choose either to despair as we focus on our failures or to flee to Christ and receive the victory He achieved for us at Calvary. In the latter case, the devil inadvertently chases us there. Satan pushes us into the arms of Jesus! After all,

> Who will bring any charge against those whom God has chosen? It is God who justifies. Who then is the one who condemns? No one. Christ Jesus who died—more than that, who was raised to life—is at the right hand of God and is also interceding for us. (Rom. 8:33–34 NIV)

God uses evil to bring judgment upon us for our own good. In many countries today, murderers and rapists are still executed for their crimes to dissuade others from committing such crimes. Soldiers kill terrorists in order to defend the innocent. God takes no pleasure in death but uses it for the greater good.

The angel of death was sent to judge the Egyptians by killing their firstborn sons. But again, all judgment, evil, and human suffering are divinely orchestrated toward holy ends: "so that the tested genuineness of your faith—more precious than gold that perishes though it is tested by fire—may be found to result in praise and glory and honor at the revelation of Jesus Christ" (1 Pet. 1:7).

Consider the example of St. Paul in his spiritual battle with the devil: "a messenger of Satan [was given] to harass me, to keep me from becoming conceited" (2 Cor. 12:7). As a matter of fact, some early interpreters of this text have argued that Paul was oppressed or even possessed by the devil as God taught this missionary, pastor, and servant indispensable life lessons. The history of Christianity is filled with stories of God permitting His saints to be violently attacked by the devil, all for His good purposes that include building and expanding His Church and her mission.

Even when Job's life became the playground of the evil one, it was all for the good of the world, so that we could learn how God is hidden in our seasons of suffering, promising to do wonderful things that exceed our imagination, even though we may need to wait for heaven to find out what those all are.

And, of course, the crucifixion of Jesus Christ is the epic manifestation of how God uses the evils of suffering for the greater good of saving the world. The only One who deserved to forgo evil experiences in life suffered the greatest of evils for us on the cross: "For our sake he made him to be sin who knew no sin, so that in him we might become the righteousness of God" (2 Cor. 5:21). Our holy Savior was handed to darkness so that the power of darkness could be destroyed once and for all.

The Devil Always Loses

You will cling tighter to Jesus in your spiritual battles with suffering and evil when you firmly believe that the devil always loses. He may look or feel like he owns the place, but he's actually acting out of eternal frustration with his destiny. His confidence is a facade. The greatest lesson learned when it comes to the ministry of deliverance is this: Don't be tempted to trust your experiences or feelings. Instead, trust Christ. Regardless of the hoped-for results, when you are faithful, you are always a victor in Him. God's Word is fulfilled in His time, not yours (Luke 1:20).

As I mentioned earlier, to stare into the eyes of a demoniac may cause you to believe that the evil one is superior. When the demons return or seem to never have departed, you will feel like a failure. Such external experiences will ultimately deceive you. Your eyes, heart, and mind will often lead you astray. Instead, you must trust only the Word of God, despite all appearances. It's when God looks like He's far away that He's actually closer to you than ever before.

In other words, you must live by faith (Rom. 1:17). When it comes to ministering to those who may struggle their whole lives with severe temptation, oppression, or possession, hold fast to the unswerving truth that your sins are forgiven in Christ and this Light of the World is present with each of us in the thickest darkness. Otherwise, you'll become immensely disappointed or even despairing when the victory expected, or for which you prayed, doesn't materialize in the way that you wished.

Jesus appeared powerless on the cross (Phil. 2:8), and yet was the power of God as "God chose what is foolish in the world to shame the wise; God chose what is weak in the world to shame the strong" (1 Cor. 1:27). Yet our God is good and has absolute control over the world. He cares for us and abides with us always until the end of the age (Matt. 28:20). You'll be glad to know that in Christ, *we* have power and authority over the devil too! Our problem is that we simply don't believe.

Although a servant, the devil is a rebel. He keeps stepping out of line and needs to be told his place. This happens by Christ's authoritative Word. No Christian would question that Jesus has full authority and power over demons (Matt. 12:28; Mark 1:27; Luke 4:36). Yet what about us as His followers? Jesus knew He wouldn't be with the disciples always. What was the "succession plan" after His ascension? As any good leader, He passed the baton of authority on to others whom He had prepared for the task: to His Church, through His disciples who then became His apostles.

When the disciples, which means "students," wanted to dismiss the congregation prior to the feeding of the five thousand at Bethsaida, Jesus's appeal to them was, "You give them something to eat" (Luke 9:13). This order was spiritually fulfilled when they took charge of His Church in obedience to His command: "Feed my sheep" (John 21:17). Loving Jesus meant responsibly putting to use the incredible authority Jesus had shared with them.

With great authority comes great power. That divine ministry continues to work through the Christian Church today, as the Holy Spirit ordains solid pastors and plants faithful congregations. Christian clergy are representatives of God's people to the world and also re-presenters of the mystical presence of Christ, who continues to abide within the temple of the Church consisting of countless biblical and Christ-centered congregations. The pastoral office is, then, an extension of our Lord's office, inasmuch as the pastor's ministry continues through laypeople in their own respective vocations after they depart a church service or Bible study: preaching, teaching, and healing broken hearts at home, work, and play.

The Role of the Church

Christ always intended to channel His power, gifts, qualities, and ministry through His Church. It's no coincidence that in Mark 1, immediately after Jesus battles the devil in the desert, the disciples are called as coworkers and students, and the first miracle is the casting out of a demon. Let us see how that account connects the work of Jesus with the Church's ministry today:

> And immediately there was in their synagogue a man with an unclean spirit. And he cried out, "What have you to do with us, Jesus of Nazareth? Have you come to destroy us? I know who you are—the Holy One of God." But Jesus rebuked him, saying, "Be silent, and come out of him!" And the unclean spirit, convulsing him and crying out with a loud voice, came out of him. And they were all amazed, so that they questioned among themselves, saying, "What is this? A new teaching with authority! He commands even the unclean spirits, and they obey him." (Mark 1:23–27)

When we unpack this text, we learn several important things. Firstly, when Jesus "rebuked" the unclean spirit, He uses the Greek word *epetimēsen* (see also 3:12; 9:25), which involves the idea of "silencing" the demon.[1] The unclean spirit is silenced because he is acting out of order, against submission to the will of God, and thus not achieving his God-given purpose as a divine tool or instrument. He's misusing or abusing his role as an angel and is ordered to stop.

Secondly, even when the demon tells the truth, calling Jesus the Holy One of God, he does it unaligned with the will of God. He speaks with evil intent. It's improper. That

---

1. It isn't surprising, then, that a version of the same word is used in His commanding: *epitassō* (Mark 1:27; see also 9:25; Luke 8:31).

word needs to be silenced at that time and that place and from that mouth. It seems to be the same reason St. Paul silences the fortune teller even when she was telling the truth (see Acts 16:16–18). The truth, in the wrong hands, doesn't always set free. There is a time and a place for everything, and God makes those decisions.

The root of the word Jesus employs in His exorcism originates from *taxis*, which literally involves "putting things back in order." So Jesus rightfully commands the spirit to get back into place and be quiet.

When Jesus is caught in the storm in Mark 4:39, He rebukes the wind and the waves with identical language, commanding them back into place, since they, too, are behaving out of order. The Hebrew version of the verb is used in the Old Testament for God's response to the threat of hostile, chaotic powers (Pss. 18:15; 76:6; 104:7; 106:9; Isa. 17:13; 50:2; Nah. 1:4). Through His word, Jesus stills the chaos, restores order, and silences the evils when they're interfering with His sovereign will and plan. Jesus's word always puts all things in right place and order.

The Role of God's Word

So how does one deal with the devil? The simple answer is with God's Word! Yet how do we receive that Word? Through His Church. God always works through physical means of getting His power, promises, and grace to us. When God became flesh, He adopted fleshly ways of abiding with us. The incarnation is a slap to the face of any gnostic tendencies we may be tempted to hold. Well, that enfleshed presence of Christ as both God *and man*—a personal union, as the ancient fathers called it, which includes the power and authority that are intrinsic to His divine and human natures—continues through the workings of the Church.

The human *mouth* of a pastor, the plain and simple *water* of holy baptism, the common *bread* and *wine* of the Lord's Supper, and the ordinary *pages* of God's extraordinary book defeat the devil day in and day out.

> Since therefore the children share in flesh and blood, he himself likewise partook of the same things, that through death he might destroy the one who has the power of death, that is, the devil, and deliver all those who through fear of death were subject to lifelong slavery. (Heb. 2:14–15)

The authority to perform works of God was given to Jesus, who then passed this authority on to His chosen disciples. These works continue through what some churches have called "the means of grace": the sacramental services, preaching, and teaching ministry of the Church (Matt. 28:18–19). Through these physical means, the Holy Spirit is powerfully at work: "But if it is by the Spirit of God that I cast out demons, then the kingdom of God has come upon you" (12:28). When Jesus institutes the Office of the Keys, handing His authority to forgive and retain sins to the Church—"If you forgive the sins of any, they are forgiven them; if you withhold forgiveness from any, it is withheld" (John 20:23)—to be administered by His ordained pastors, this also includes the ability to free people from unclean spirits. Those whom the devil binds, Jesus frees (Luke 13:16). Jesus lends His authority to pastors to continue to bind "the dragon" (Rev. 20:2) or "the strong man" (Matt. 12:29), so to speak, so people can be liberated to follow Jesus. That's one reason why, as we'll discuss in the next chapter, I believe "exorcism" isn't an ability given exclusively to a few select individuals but rather a function of the pastoral office. It's a gift given to all believers, through the Church and her orders. In this sense, every legitimate pastor is an "exorcist," though most have no experience in this area at all.

Faithful Christian Community

Don't be mistaken. This divine ministry isn't limited to clergy. Pastors and laypeople employ the gospel in different places and ways. The pastors feed the sheep, who then feed the world. The Word of the Lord then grows by being spread. Even when laypeople provide spiritual support that normally would involve pastors, they aren't simply operating with individual faith in Christ but also on behalf of the larger Church. They, too, have the company of heaven on their side.

Yet God has established an order, and the exceptions should not replace the rule. Baptisms can be conducted by laypeople, but only in an emergency. When it comes to exorcism, let this be a warning to all Christians never to tackle these special cases alone. Pastors and congregations must work together. Even though the ministry of deliverance is conducted under the auspice and direction of Christian leaders, who hold the apostolic office on behalf of their congregations within the larger Church order, the work presumes the prayers of the members, counsel from the most wise and faithful, and a loving Christian community that welcomes all sinners, including recovering tax collectors, prostitutes, and even demoniacs, into their church and worship life. "No man should be alone when he opposes Satan. The Church and the ministry of the Word were instituted for this purpose, that hands may be joined together and help each other. If the prayer of one doesn't help, the prayer of another will."[2] The Bible emphasizes corporate intercession for pastors and missionaries (Eph. 6:18–19; 2 Thess. 3:1–3) and for all those in positions of authority, so that together all servants serve the church rather than Satan (1 Tim. 2:1–6).

The ministry of deliverance assumes teamwork. Never forget: No follower of Jesus, whether pastor, priest, or layperson, *is* Jesus. Yes, Jesus lives in Christians, as St. Paul states: "I have been crucified with Christ and I no longer live, but Christ lives in me. The life I now live in the body, I live by faith in the Son of God, who loved me and gave himself for me" (Gal. 2:20 NIV). We are His earthen vessels (2 Cor. 4:6–7) since Christ has made a home in our hearts, where He actively dwells today (Eph. 3:17).

So in a sense, in Christ, you are authorized to speak that performative Word of Jesus as Jesus operates through you. Yet that ministry happens with conditions. For instance, we want to avoid confusing our will with God's will, as we pray in the Lord's Prayer. Jesus's will is always God's will because He is both man *and God*, unlike us. We don't have full knowledge of the divine plan. God's good and perfect answers to our prayers often disappoint us for that very reason. When you use the Word in the ministry of deliverance, you must use it carefully and prayerfully. You don't grab it for yourself like the sons of Sceva (Acts 19:13–14) but rather let God produce the results according to His Word and will.

Moses didn't intend to abuse his power when he struck the rock, yet he displeased God, even though the water flowed (Num. 20:10–13). The tool that had been entrusted to him still worked, even though it had been abused. This is both a comfort and a warning for us. We need never doubt the

2. Martin Luther, *Luther's Works, Volume 54: Table Talk* (Fortress Press, 1967), 78.

effectiveness of the tools entrusted to us in ministry. Our sins are forgiven even if an unbelieving pastor speaks the words. God's Word is powerful in itself, "like the roar of many waters" (Rev. 1:15). That is how much God wants to ensure we receive them. But woe to the one who speaks them wrongfully! We pastors must constantly assess our own intentions and use of God's Word as it is applied throughout our various life vocations. We are "stewards of the mysteries of God" (1 Cor. 4:1). These mysteries, or "sacraments" in Latin, don't belong to us. They belong to the King, and we are mere servants. The moment we try to reverse those roles by having a domineering attitude or behaving like we are in charge, we've made the error of the demons.

Praying versus Commandeering

A good example of the idea of submission of our will to God's while attempting to deliver those from demonic oppression or possession involves the age-old question among exorcists as to whether they are authorized to commandeer demons—ordering their departure—or must simply pray for the demoniac's deliverance.

Certainly, in the historical rites of holy baptism, an order for the devil to flee from the candidate is declared: "Depart, unclean spirit, and make way for the Holy Spirit." Yet such sacraments have the clear command and promise of God attached to them. God orders us to do them and promises certain results. When it comes to exorcisms, we only have descriptions in the Bible of how they were performed. In other words, we have, at best, some divinely inspired guidelines but no command or promise.

During the Reformation era, there was an upswing of recorded exorcisms, and Martin Luther and the Roman

Catholics fought tooth and nail over how to interpret the data. Rational reasoning was often clouded by a lot of mud-slinging. On the one hand, Roman Catholic priests basically denied that Protestant exorcisms were successful. They claimed that they had a monopoly on such abilities through the authority of the pope. On the other hand, when Luther heard about priests exorcising demons using liturgical rites, he would argue that they were just showing off and that the devil liked a good ceremony.[3]

Luther argued, instead, that prayer was the only way to address them. Remember Paul and the thorn in his side? He addressed it with prayer. The logic was, as hard as it may be to believe, that sometimes it's God's will that we don't receive the hoped-for answers to our prayers. After all, often in life we think we're praying for bread but are actually asking for a scorpion (Luke 11:11–13). So God denies our prayer in His profound mystery and hidden will.

We may pray for a little baby dying from a terminal illness who still dies. We may pray for the healing of a cancer patient and be disappointed with the outcome. We haven't been provided with the answers to all life's questions, for our own good. In heaven, there will be complete healing. But on earth, we don't have that promise. Jesus healed the sick and raised the dead, and yet those people all still eventually died.

When it comes to demonism, we pray for deliverance, yet the person may still suffer for years with the same condition. I exorcised one woman more times than I can remember. She struggled unto her death with those demons. Yet in hindsight I believe she wouldn't have remained Christian and would have released her clutch of Christ's cross if not for

3. Benjamin Mayes, "Demonic Possession and Exorcism in Lutheran Orthodoxy," *Concordia Theological Quarterly* 81 (2017): 334–35.

her ongoing struggle. For every time the demon reappeared, she would race to the Church or call the pastor for ministry. Even on her deathbed, the demon verbally assaulted the pastor. After the pastor silenced it, she happily invited him to proceed with last rites.

Prayer leaves all choices in the hands of God. Sometimes it's God's will that there's no deliverance at the moment. Jesus Himself says that some demons only come out through prayer (Mark 9:29). Yet at the same time, we do have biblical precedent for rebuking demons by commanding them to leave. We are to do so in a prayerful way, leaving all results to God's sovereign direction.

Even Martin Luther, in spite of his criticisms of commandeering demons, was known for speaking to the devil, in mockery, and even writing hymns rebuking him verbally. We all live in contradiction. But Luther was absolutely right: We must trust the Lord rather than our works or experiences. And only prayer allows us to do that.

Looks can be deceiving. Sometimes a demon can pretend to leave the demoniac temporarily or even verbally admit defeat while actually still remaining present and in control, playing games with the Christians with evil purposes in mind. Also, the devil likes attention, which is why many have criticized elaborate exorcisms that seem to put on a good show, entertaining the company of hell with all the fancy rites and ceremonies. So focusing on our own ability to exorcise demons and the fruits thereof can be a dangerous business. The power needs to be Christ's and not ours. "Thy will be done."

Personally, I rebuke and command demons, but I do it prayerfully and with careful discernment. I don't know any other way. When I have time to prepare, I prefer to use historical rites that are reliable and proven over the test of time, such as the famous Roman Ritual and other biblical and historical liturgies, but I am by no means tied to those in any legalistic ways.

Like the holy angels and people, each demon is different. So they don't all react in the same way to the same weapons and tools. Christians need to be flexible and navigate carefully and humbly when dealing with them during an exorcism, relying on the wisdom of the Holy Spirit. They need to ensure biblical texts are central to whatever material is used. The holy name, words, and works of Jesus the Lord and Savior are central to the intervention.

The ministry of deliverance for the demon-possessed can sometimes resemble a kind of superstitious reading of spells by Christian witch doctors when it isn't fueled by faith and prayer. There's no room for mocking demons out of spite, interviewing them out of curiosity, or inviting spectators to join you in the spectacle. Immature faith or puffed-up egos will sabotage the ability to decide the right balance between commandeering and prayer.

Prayer during an exorcism is like calling the cops while you hold a thief who broke into your house at gunpoint. You don't chitchat or invite your friends over to see what you have trapped. You concentrate on forcing them to leave, holding your weapon with one hand while calling the police with the other, patiently waiting for the authorities' direction.

The Salvation of Souls

As evidence of being followers of Jesus, and the continuation of the ministry established by the Father who sent His Son who, in turn, sent the apostles, the apostles performed both spiritual and physical miracles, including binding Satan and the demons (Matt. 12:29) and loosing spiritual prisoners from their captivity (Luke 13:16; see also Mark 7:35).

Jesus's commission to the Twelve for the practice of the ministry of deliverance is demonstrated by their power over physical ailments as well as spiritual ones:

> He called to him his twelve disciples and gave them authority over unclean spirits, to cast them out, and to heal every disease and every affliction. . . . "And proclaim as you go, saying, 'The kingdom of heaven is at hand.' Heal the sick, raise the dead, cleanse lepers, cast out demons." (Matt. 10:1, 7–8)

Physical and spiritual healing were found side by side in their ministry, as virtually each incident of deliverance recorded in the New Testament involved preaching and proclaiming the Word of God and the gospel (Mark 1:39; 3:14–15; Luke 9:2).

The two tasks go hand in hand. But spiritual deliverance takes precedence over the physical, as Jesus Himself reminds the Pharisees who criticize His comforting proclamation to the paralytic: "'Which is easier, to say, "Your sins are forgiven," or to say, "Rise and walk"? But that you may know that the Son of Man has authority on earth to forgive sins'—he then said to the paralytic—'Rise, pick up your bed and go home'" (Matt. 9:5–6). Miracles are never intended to simply make life more bearable. They're always meant to increase faith in Jesus Christ as the Savior from sin, eternal death, and the devil. The point of all Christian ministry is the salvation of souls through the forgiveness of sins. Jesus's Word, and the authority He lends to us, always has that eternal goal in mind.

The Greatest Act of Deliverance

Some question the continuity between the authority and ministry of the Church yesterday and today. They wonder whether twenty-first-century pastors have authority over the demonic world. Although pastors aren't apostles, they stand in apostolic succession. They hold the same faith and are servants of the same Lord. They're of the same lineage inasmuch as all Christians belong to the same nation: the spiritual Israel.

Jesus's gift of authority to the seventy evangelists to trample demons and the power of the enemy (Luke 10:19) wasn't offered just to them but to the whole Church and to be practiced by the larger team of ministers. Jesus corrected His disciples' prejudice on the question of any one group of people having "exclusive rights" to our Lord's authority.

> John said to him, "Teacher, we saw someone casting out demons in your name, and we tried to stop him, because he was not following us." But Jesus said, "Do not stop him, for no one who does a mighty work in my name will be able soon afterward to speak evil of me. For the one who is not against us is for us." (Mark 9:38–40)

There's no doubt about it. The apostles held a special and unique place in the kingdom of God, and their role was different from ours—but our mission today is the same. The military consists of generals and privates, specialists and supporters, yet all fight the same war. In the Lord's army, "He gave the apostles, the prophets, the evangelists, the shepherds and teachers, to equip the saints for the work of ministry, for building up the body of Christ" (Eph. 4:11–12).

Today, faithful Christian clergy carry on the functions of the apostolic ministry and with the same authority. For example, the apostles were given the authority to forgive sins in the stead of God Himself: "And when he had said this, he breathed on them and said to them, 'Receive the Holy Spirit. If you forgive the sins of any, they are forgiven them; if you withhold forgiveness from any, it is withheld'" (John 20:22–23). Pastors do the same today. They do it from the pulpit, and they do it as part of individual care and counseling.

They may not necessarily perform physical miracles, but some do, especially missionaries in the untouched pockets of the world. All perform spiritual miracles, such as baptism and celebrating the Lord's Supper, and other ways of creating faith and healing hearts through biblical and Christlike shepherding. Jesus promises this: "Truly, truly, I say to you, whoever believes in me will also do the works that I do; and greater works than these will he do, because I am going to the Father" (John 14:12).

The most important miracles are never temporal. Invisible ones yield fruit for eternity. Any visible miracles are always aimed at pointing people to that heavenly vineyard. There's no greater blessing on earth than knowing that your prayers have been heard by almighty God, and that He will answer them according to His good and gracious will. The fact that God remains flesh and dwells among us and lives within us is truly supernatural. Salvation is the greatest of miracles.

> The seventy-two returned with joy, saying, "Lord, even the demons are subject to us in your name!" And he said to them, "I saw Satan fall like lightning from heaven. Behold, I have given you authority to tread on serpents and scorpions, and over all the power of the enemy, and nothing shall hurt you. Nevertheless, do not rejoice in this, that the spirits are subject to you, but rejoice that your names are written in heaven." (Luke 10:17–20)

All Christians handle the serpents of sin, death, and the devil whenever they remember that God has made them His dear and precious children through baptism and faith, and when they proclaim the Word and the gospel. For "now is the judgment of this world; now will the ruler of this world be cast out" (John 12:31). The devil's kingdom is severely assaulted every time sins are forgiven and a soul is saved (Luke 15:7).

Ultimately, the worst situation for a person isn't living with demon possession on earth but a possession of hell in the afterlife. At the end of the day, the only thing that sinks us to Hades is the weight of our sin and unbelief. Yet God graciously releases us and frees us by the forgiveness purchased and won at Calvary through His victorious Son. That is the greatest act of deliverance!

A Pastoral Responsibility to Care for Souls

Pastors aren't promised the same kinds of miraculous abilities as were given to the apostles. These early clergy had a hard job proving themselves as legitimate servants of the Messiah and the Maker of heaven and earth since the Bible hadn't yet been compiled and canonized. Miracles provided the evidence that they were who they said they were. Yet we are better off today. His grace is sufficient for us (2 Cor. 12:9) as we stand on the shoulders of these apostolic giants.

Although some of the apostles' abilities were restricted to the apostolic age, others do still apply to us today. Jesus's commission of the apostles with His own authority and power to cast out demons (Matt. 10:1; Mark 3:15; 6:7; Luke 9:1) includes us.

Most pastors are understandably apprehensive addressing demonism. They would rather send those with demonic symptoms to a local medical doctor, psychiatrist, or social worker than confront these issues themselves. These secular professionals have their places, but, in themselves, they aren't the solutions. By trade, they cannot address the spiritual source that is the core of demonism, even when manifested physically. Pharmaceuticals can sometimes help, but they, too, are not enough.

So just like pastors can't just avoid visiting the dying in a hospital because they don't believe they are skilled in palliative care, they can't refer those suffering with demonic issues to others due to doubts that they are unable to help more. Certainly, we all have our gifts, and some pastors are better at grief ministry while others are more talented with youth. But pastors' basic obligations to care for the souls of all their people include addressing this unusual spiritual illness and not just handing over uncomfortable situations to strangers. "God is faithful; he will not let you be tempted beyond what you can bear. But when you are tempted, he will also provide a way out so that you can endure it" (1 Cor. 10:13 NIV). We never have a reason to fear. The Christian approach to faith is always framed in this way: "I believe; help my unbelief!" (Mark 9:24). God doesn't want cocky followers who forget that they are servants and behave like kings. It's an honor to suffer for the Lord, which often happens through getting tangled up in other people's problems. And demonism is just one of countless ways the devil tries to wreck the lives of God's children: no better, no worse. When you realize that, you won't make such a big deal about manifestations of the demonic. You won't be surprised. You'll stop being curious. You'll realize that the devil fears those who no longer fear him. When I accept an invitation to participate in an exorcism, my attitude is this: "Let's just get this done and over with . . . and keep the debrief short."

In short, exorcism isn't just the function of a specialist. While some may be more at ease in this domain than others, the Holy Spirit equips all pastors to do everything required to succeed in His ministry, including dealing with demons. God is capable and will do it, for He "is able to do far more abundantly than all that we ask or think" (Eph. 3:20).

After all, even though the family car belongs to all the members of the household and isn't the possession of just one person, there can only be one designated driver. Jesus has trained and chosen His pastors for that unique position, though all the riders have a role to play, too, as God uses the hands, feet, eyes, and mouths of each. One navigates, another finds the right tunes to play, and yet another passes out the snacks or leads the group in some fun-filled activities when the journey is long.

This analogy isn't perfect, and maybe it's even a little silly, but when it comes to the Christian congregation, there's got to be one designated leader who takes responsibility. Their "driver's license" of ordination testifies to an adequate level of training, confidence, and comfort, as well as the authorization. Yet unfortunately, not all theological topics are covered in seminary. In fact, most seminaries avoid the topic of exorcism. So if pastors feel ill-equipped to drive on this road, they may sometimes need to delegate the driver's seat to one of the passengers. Yet they are still in charge.

Pastors aren't just Q&A theologians or those who conduct religious ceremonies. They're expected to feed their sheep in holistic ways (John 21:15–17), which are cultivated by taking an interest in the lives of their people and through building loving and trusting relationships. They may not always like what they find, especially when forced to explore some pretty dark places, but those are precisely the areas that need special attention. Like anything, the first time is hard, but God is with us until the end of the age (Matt. 28:20).

5

KINDS AND SYMPTOMS OF DEMONISM

There are two kinds of "possession," one spiritual and one physical. They are intertwined. Our internal battles with lust, greed, or pride often involve decisions that we make with our hands, mouths, and eyes. But the difference between a physical possession and a spiritual one is that in the former one loses complete control over both body and faculties for a period of time. Physical possession is rare. The devil uses one's flesh, even temporarily, as a conduit for his own intent and personality. He becomes the puppeteer. Yet the level of control is a matter of degree, and there is some gray area. Demonic oppression involves the presence of the devil in one's body and life, but not in the sense of the host losing complete control.

Because of the cooperative nature of demonic oppression, it can be difficult to detect. Although there are many differences between cases along the wide spectrum of demonic oppression to possession, some clear commonalities exist.

Knowing this helps in caring for all those poor suffering souls, no matter where they fall on the grid. Principles of operation within this unexplored terrain derive from five key New Testament texts on demonism, which we'll refer to as "the Big Five":

The man in the synagogue in Capernaum
  (Mark 1:21–28).

The Gerasene man with a legion of demons
  (Mark 5:1–20).

The daughter of the Syrophoenician woman
  (Mark 7:24–30).

The father whose son had an impure spirit (Mark
  9:14–29).

The crippled woman on the Sabbath (Luke 13:10–17).

When carefully examining these important accounts of our Lord performing exorcism, we discover some shared features that give us guidelines as to how to practice the ministry of deliverance today.

Firstly, there's no single pattern or procedure, implying that there's considerable freedom in practicing and responding, albeit within a rigid framework as will become evident.

Secondly, Jesus is always the exorcist. And Jesus is always found linked to His Word. Jesus uses God's performative Word to cast out demons. Recall how Jesus rebuked the devil in the desert during His demonic temptations. He quoted Scripture. We ought to avoid creative efforts when it comes to the devil and just stick to the old-fashioned Word of God in our rebukes.

Thirdly, power over the darkness is exclusively experienced through an encounter with Jesus the Christ. Jesus stands with us also. The obvious and critical way of accessing this source of power is prayer, which is simply talking to Jesus. Consider the effect of the humble intercession by the Phoenician woman for her daughter. Reflect upon the father bringing his demonically possessed son to Jesus in Mark 9:29, where Jesus said, "This kind cannot be driven out by anything but prayer."

Through prayer, Jesus graciously shares His power with us. Even better, He shares His authority over the dark realm with us. Which brings us to the last shared point in the Big Five texts: All of them emphasize that the Word and Christ's teaching have authority from heaven. The Church, and the weapons with which He has entrusted her, continue to win victories in the battlefield today. No matter how small your church, "God is [your] refuge and strength" (Ps. 46:1), and it is a mighty fortress, an embassy of heaven. It's filled with ambassadors who deliver God's Word and communicate with heaven through prayer. "Therefore, we are ambassadors for Christ, God making his appeal through us" (2 Cor. 5:20).

Manifestations of the demonic are not occasions for panic but are opportunities to pray. The devil hates being the cause of our prayers! One young man was delivered after a congregation of his friends held a prayer vigil for him. They came to the realization that he was not just going through a rebellious phase in his adolescence but that his character had been radically altered for quite some time. That evening, the boy "regained consciousness" and claimed that he had not known his whereabouts for several months. He said it was like waking up from a long sleep. Prayer matters.

A friend of mine talked about marching in a pro-life parade in St. Louis. Pro-choice protesters arrived in zombie costumes determined to frighten children. They shouted profanities and behaved in other intimidating ways against these peaceful Christians. A pastor started to speak the Litany, an ancient prayer that includes petitions for peace. Immediately, the badgering and verbal violence stopped. The protesters quietly walked away. Prayer matters.

Returning, then, to the earlier question about whether we are authorized only to pray or can also commandeer demons: I'm increasingly convinced that boldly deploying the performative Word of Jesus while praying at the same time are entirely reconcilable—when we're focused on Jesus as the chief exorcist who has loaned us His authority and power. But when this focus gets blurred at any point in our battles, by lack of faith or faltering prayers, we always fail. This usually happens by pride, egoism, or self-righteousness. When we drift away from Christ as our anchor, we get lost in uncharted seas. These are vast, perilous places. And even though God is good, and can bring us back, the ministry gets a lot harder than it needs to be.

Consider the disciples in Mark 9, who were puzzled by their inability to cast out certain demons. Early biblical manuscripts record Jesus informing the disappointed disciples that those demons could only be exorcised by "fasting and prayer." Many read this to mean that if the disciples had just done that one extra thing—fasting—to strengthen themselves, they would have been successful. But I wonder if what was really going on is that the disciples were getting a little too confident in themselves. What fasting preaches to us is this: "Don't look to yourself for power. Look to Jesus. He is the strong One who has overcome the world." Fasting exposes our weakness, not our strength. How many of us are in a better mood when we're hungry or perkier after having deprived ourselves of shopping for a season or from the internet for even a day? Nobody looks prettier or feels stronger in sackcloth and ashes, neither physically nor spiritually. True Christian fasting, as an expression of a humble faith toward God and love toward one another, doesn't turn us inward upon ourselves—where the problem is—but outward, toward God.[1]

That being said, there's no excuse for weak and lazy warriors. God's forgiveness doesn't free us to sin more. "By no means! How can we who died to sin still live in it?" (Rom. 6:2). Instead, it frees and enables us to serve God and our neighbor in new and greater ways. It liberates us to fight harder against the evil one.

I know a married Christian man who has struggled his entire life with masturbation. God forgives him whenever he slips up, but, like a football athlete who regrets breaking his healthy diet by gorging on fast food, he's weaker for it even though he doesn't lose his status or position in the field. When we were baptized, we became spiritual athletes (vv. 3–4), no matter our age, and "every athlete exercises self-control in all things" (1 Cor. 9:25). We are called to discipline ourselves and to keep our lives under control so that we can be of good use in the spiritual battle. In the ministry of deliverance, the practitioner needs to be spiritually fit. There's no room for the conceited and presumptuous. Instead, "Let the one who boasts, boast in the Lord" (2 Cor. 10:17).

Symptoms of Physical Possession

Many assume that prior to the modern age and the scientific revolution, everyone was superstitious, illogical, and unreasonable. This is simply untrue and exhibits unfounded prejudice. There really is nothing new under the sun (Eccles. 1:9), and that includes worldviews.

1. Harold Ristau, "Tempted to Fast?," *The Lutheran Witness*, March 2020, 11–12.

When it comes to demonism, we find that even in the Middle Ages the ministry of deliverance was being practiced responsibly. One of the first questions clergy asked was whether demonic symptoms could be attributed to mental illness. Today in Rome, exorcists at the Vatican work closely in collaboration with the medical community in cases where there's a clear crossover between mental and spiritual health. A writing by a sixteenth-century German pastor named Friedrich Balduin provides a practical tool for pastors when navigating through these sorts of questions. He even categorized symptoms as "primary" versus "secondary," demonstrating a very methodological, systematic, and thus *scientific* approach to the discerning of spirits (1 John 4:1–6). He wasn't atypical. And we basically use the same kind of instruments for diagnosis today. He writes:

> One must be careful not to mistake demon possession for a natural disease. Some symptoms which are sometimes mistaken are ecstasy, epileptic seizures, lethargy, insanity, frantic state of mind, and similar conditions. Convulsions and stupendous bodily movements should not be assumed to be demon possession. These sorts of symptoms could stem from purely natural causes, or could be partially assisted by the devil.[2]

Secret Knowledge

Balduin continues by listing clear symptoms of true possession. The knowledge of things the person couldn't possibly have known is an obvious one. One young boy, after a demon took residence in him, knew the whereabouts

2. Friedrich Balduin, *Tractatus de casibus conscientiae* (1636), trans. Benjamin Mayes, "Demon Possession and Exorcism in Lutheran Orthodoxy," *Concordia Theological Quarterly*, July–October 2017, 332–33. Used by permission.

of objects in his home that were hidden by his parents. Another sign is the ability to engage in diverse and foreign language. The demons have had thousands of years to learn languages and acquire information. It's no wonder that they can easily share their expertise with their hosts. I, personally, have often heard them speak with foreign accents. In one of my cases, a poor English speaker, when possessed, sounded like a kid from New Jersey. It even convinced a skeptic who happened to be in the room that his buddy was unquestionably and directly under the influence of Satan.

On another occasion, I dealt with someone on the phone who was struggling with severe demonic oppression. In the midst of my prayers, I spoke the Lord's Prayer. I have often snuck the Our Father into counseling sessions with such people in order to get a reaction through which I can then assess the degree of oppression. That prayer in particular usually aggravates the demons in drastic ways. In this case, I decided to pray it in German. Suddenly, the man began mocking me in perfect German, saying, "You don't think I know German?" I silenced him, in English.

Claiming to receive messages from nonhuman entities is a major proof of supernatural demonic presence. Children under demonic influence are often very forthcoming with this kind of information. After all, children are especially susceptible to demonic forces because they're so trusting. Parents understand this when it comes to interacting with strangers and schoolmates. They want to keep their children safe from harm and are rightly cautious due to a child's vulnerability. They shouldn't, therefore, roll their eyes at children's stories about evil entities visiting them in their heads, in their dreams, or when nobody else is around. Some of this may be attributed to their imagination, but that shouldn't be the default position when they are regular occurrences. If it turns out that there are demons involved, there's no reason to panic. Christ is Victor, and all these concerns can be addressed with prayer and the Word. But adopting a dismissive attitude is careless.

Frankly, an even greater threat to their spiritual well-being is the kinds of information to which kids are exposed. With the increase of anti-Christian ideologies in schools and media of all sorts, parents should be carefully monitoring what their children are learning. Children whose spiritual lives may have been compromised by the neglect of such oversight, coupled by other thoughtless parental practices, are more prone to be targeted by diabolical influences. Drawings or sketches of what children have seen in dreams and heard from imaginary friends should be of concern if other symptoms are also present.

I have been involved in several cases where evil notes were found in unfamiliar handwriting in a child's room, with messages intended to terrify parents as opposed to frighten children. In one case, the faithful Christian father simply shrugged his shoulders and responded, "It proves I must be doing something right, if the devil takes such interest in my family." He had a good attitude. After all, for those in Christ, the devil is all bite with no teeth.

The innocence of young children makes them more resilient than adults. And their openness and eagerness to trust means children will also listen to parents' solutions, unlike adolescents or teenagers who are more prone to resist. But for young children, as quickly as the evil can enter, it can exit, given the right spiritual program. One note that a parent found on the writing desk of their four-year-old son was, "I will kill him." Such intimidation tactics, though terrifying, are easily combated when we accept that the devil is a liar who is harmless before the children of God. The family began daily evening prayers and hymn singing in the son's bedroom, which seemed to chase those demons away.

Don't be surprised that the demons know a lot about your life. The demonically oppressed will often claim to have secret knowledge about future events. Demons are watching us all over the world. This, coupled with efficient networks of communication, doesn't make them all-knowing, but it does make them thousands of times more knowing than humans. This is why they can appear to predict the future (Acts 16:16) even though they don't actually know the future. Instead, they have maximum access to information and present circumstances to make accurate predictions about many future events. If someone was listening in on all your phone conversations, would it be a surprise that they'd gathered a pretty good picture of what your weekend plans were?

Although there are as many charlatans as there are real practitioners, palm reading, tarot cards, horoscopes, most yoga practices, and the like should be off the table for any serious Christian. Consider the police using people who allegedly have ESP to track down lost people or things. Demons don't mind being put to some "good" use but always with sinister results in the long run. Witching rods used to find water underground are an example of tapping into supernatural forces and should be avoided until or unless a logical explanation is one day discovered. No technology is morally neutral. Christians should be wary of AI, particularly when the robot seems personable, flaunting the ability to relate to you as a human being. Once you dabble in the secret arts of the dark one, even inadvertently, you have opened a door, an entry point, for yourself and your loved ones through which the demons may now enter.

The degrees of evil influence vary from person to person and case to case, and so do the consequences. For instance, I had a friend whose Registered Massage Therapist practiced the New Age art of Reiki on his body. Incidentally, although she claimed to be a Christian, she couldn't utter the name of Jesus. She exhibited personal autonomy except when it came to articulating her religious convictions. Similarly, in the case of ESP, the evil spirit is assisting and not necessarily possessing the person bodily. Yet don't kid yourself; the demon can take full control whenever it wishes. But in the meantime the person will have more autonomy in life than, say, mediums who offer their bodies as portals to the underworld. Mediums become like an enfleshed Ouija board. The evil presence allows them to think that they are in control of their lives, while they are actually slaves to the devil.

A fortune teller is essentially a medium. They admit that they ask for help from a spirit guide in their ventures to communicate with the dead. There's no reason to believe the ghost of Samuel summoned by the wicked witch of Endor (1 Sam. 28) wasn't actually his spirit, although some have proposed it was an impostor like a demon. If it was his "ghost," the Bible doesn't share why God permitted him to speak, but we know that the summoning was wrong and resulted in great evil. No good comes when we allow the devil to take control of our lives.

Supernatural Power

Related to this superhuman ability to determine the future through the workings of the devil is the granting of certain powers or help from Satan. I had seminary students in Kenya who needed to be persuaded that the local witch doctor's solutions to illnesses were not an option even though they were cheaper than medicine from the local drugstore. Voodoo is attractive because it's a quick fix. Getting help from the dark side may even be well intended, a way of doing some good in the short run. But what may appear altruistic is short-lived. Insecure, desperate, gullible, and selfish people are then tempted to make deals with the devil.

Lucifer is very ready to sign such contracts, exchanging material riches, worldly powers, and temporal successes for souls. Rock stars are renowned for this. Unsurprisingly, it always ends in tragedy and usually death. Successful celebrities who've claimed ties with the occult for gathering inspiration and information include Jimmy Page, Alice Cooper, Mick Jagger, John Lennon, and David Bowie.[3] Legend has it that Robert Johnson met the devil and gave him his soul in exchange for mastery of the guitar. The circumstances around his death remain a mystery.

Fortunately, contracts with the devil can be broken. One Christian youngster was healed of her illness after a satanic pact was made and inscribed on a piece of paper that she carried in an amulet around her neck. After repentance, she was delivered from the demonic oppression and destroyed the object, even though her illness returned. She held no regrets.[4] She understood that God has a purpose for suffering and that health, just like fame, can get in the way of salvation. Every devilish plan backfires in Satan's face whenever we commend our downcast spirits into Jesus's holy hands, trusting in His infinite mercy.

3. Ward Hazel, "Top 10 Musicians Who Sold Their Soul to the Devil," Listverse, September 24, 2020, https://listverse.com/2020/09/24/10-musicians-who-sold-their-soul-to-the-devil/.

4. Kurt E. Koch, *Occult Bondage and Deliverance* (Kregel, 1970), 116.

Discovery of Evil Objects

The discovery of "evil objects," such as statues that symbolize anti-Christian ideas, as well as books or recordings with unholy content, can be a sign of demonic presence when other symptoms are evident in the lives of those who own them. After an exorcism, a thorough housecleaning avails the opportunity to rid the space of any questionable objects and rededicate it to the Lord.

Unless lyrics are blatantly anti-Christian or ungodly, Christians need to decide whether it's tolerable to listen to songs produced by unbelieving artists. Musicians who are atheists can still produce lovely songs. The devil gets no credit. We're all created in the image of our beautiful Creator, and in spite of original sin that has corrupted all dimensions of human existence, the creation continues to display the wonderful fingerprints and craftsmanship of God everywhere.

Yet there are no neutral mediums of communication, as philosophers Neil Postman and Marshall McLuhan have so convincingly argued: "the medium is the message."[5] Accordingly, Christians ought to take prayerful consideration as to what degree they're willing to support artists who are anti-Christian. In making such determinations, Christians should be highly attentive to products and art that are dedicated to the evil one, or those consecrated to dark purposes.

Unfortunately, normally you don't have much information about the life of the artist whose paintings hang in your house or whose music you prefer. You'll never know the state of the heart and soul of a craftsperson who has sold you

5. See, for example, Pastor Ryun, "'The Medium Is the Message' (Marshall McLuhan)," Acts Ministries International, June 24, 2020, https://amichurches.com/blog/2020/06/24/the-medium-is-the-message-marshall-mcluhan.

some gorgeous furniture. I counseled a family who was able to identify sea salt from the Himalayas that seemed to be the source of a haunting in their house. When it was removed, the evil presence disappeared. I'm not implying that all imported food products may be inherently evil. But that batch of salt seemed to be, due to a peculiar history. The more I've been immersed in this ministry, the more sensitive I've become to such oddities. I've come to judge with new eyes the kinds of books on my shelves and objects decorating my walls. I once had a collection of exotic ceramic masks that I threw out after discovering their occult connection. Even though Christ is King over everything we own, we shouldn't keep things we'd be ashamed to show our Lord if He visited our home. We need to be careful not to abuse the freedom we have in Christ (1 Cor. 10:23). Antinomianism represents one temptation, and legalism another.

Some Christians will claim that halal meat ought never be consumed for this reason, as it is blessed by Muslim religious leaders. Eating it is arguably a participation in their religious rites. Yet this begs the question whether Christians trapped in Muslim countries where there's no choice but to consume such meats are doomed. Do North Americans realize that much food in urban restaurants and even on airplanes is halal? Have you ever noticed a statue of Buddha or Ganesh behind the counter at an Asian restaurant? Did it stop you from dining there?

There comes a point when responsible Christians must simply rely on the mercy of God, remembering that we are protected by a mighty and gracious Savior from all these unavoidable and unknown evil influences (1 Cor. 10:18–20). We are all tangled together in a society consisting of both believers and unbelievers. Meat sacrificed to idols should not frighten those who have faith in Christ, who preserves and protects our souls and bodies. Yet decisions still need to be deliberately and carefully made, and ones edifying to neighbors as in 1 Corinthians 8:1–13. Just because there's a lot of gray in the world, and we can't live perfectly consistent lives, doesn't mean we can become lazy in our decision-making. The Bible never said it would be easy to live in the secularized and pagan world around us. But it promises that the grace of God goes with us. We have no reason to fear.

Supernatural Phenomena

We cannot deny that the devil has power to influence physical material, and this should put us all on guard when it comes to evidence of the occult detected in the world around us. But Satan's demonstrations of the supernatural cannot compare with the Lord's.

When Pharaoh's magicians attempted to imitate the miracle of Moses, their snakes were swallowed up by the one God gave Moses (Exod. 7:8–13). Unlike the *Prince of Egypt* animated film that presents the witches as performing silly magic stunts, there's no reason to believe these weren't legitimate acts of witchcraft. They were real snakes summoned by satanic arts. Witch doctors have power. Yet God overcame them. Moses's snake consumed all the others, pointing clearly to how our Lord Jesus Christ, lifted on the pole of the cross, would consume the snakes of sin, death, and hell. After all, it's no coincidence that later in the wilderness, when God punished the Israelites for their rebellion with venomous snakes, gazing upon a bronze serpent lifted high on a pole was the only antidote. Jesus associates Himself with that snake.

Wherever Christ is found, the enemy is nearby. He is a poor imitator but still effective. And he carries with him a

110

sack full of tricks: a demonic version of Christ's good gifts. The black mass, for instance, is an upside-down version of the true mass. Satanic rituals are disgusting and twisted versions of Christian worship. The devil manipulates and, like a monkey in mockery of humans, *apes* our Lord. Although unconvincing to a mature Christian, it's the best he can do, since he cannot create anything himself.

Supernatural powers aren't only external to the demoniac but may also find an origin within them. Supernatural strength is common (Mark 5:2–3) and is included in the list of irregular events surrounding the demoniac. This is why exorcists have sometimes tied down their patients, although this necessity is more rare than sensationalist Hollywood movies make it out to be.

The evil one is normally quickly and easily subjected to the Word of God when spoken by the faithful, as God's holy angels join the battle on behalf of all true Christians in attendance. It may take a long time to get rid of the demon, who will always resist, but deliverance is inevitable.

One reason why the demoniac "Robbie," in the true story upon which the movie *The Exorcist* was based, had such a rough time is that Robbie was unbaptized. He had no faith, or at least lacked a faith anchored in the promises and works of Jesus. Similarly, a situation in the book of Acts describes a failed exorcism: "the man in whom was the evil spirit leaped on them, mastered all of them and overpowered them" (19:16). Here, too, this defeat can clearly be attributed to the lack of faith in the exorcists, who weren't Christians. They believed that simply uttering sacred phrases was sufficient, instead of recognizing that the words must proceed from believing hearts.

Some demons will torment bodies. In extreme cases, unusual injuries of the body are evident. In one of my cases, a contorted evil smile of the demoniac tried to intimidate me to give up the fight, while in another a childlike body posture coupled with a whiny plea for mercy tried to convince me to have sympathy for it and let it stay. I was almost tricked by its pitiful display of physical vulnerability and fragility. Sometimes those aroused from nightmares or trances suffer wounds, like bruises around wrists as if something or someone grabbed them tightly. For Robbie, this was common.

There have been instances of extraordinary motion of bodies, such as an elderly man who, being demon-possessed, was able to run as fast as a horse. I served as the pastor of a demonically possessed man who, after an exorcism, lost the specialized skills of his trade. He was a pro golfer. But after deliverance, he couldn't swing a club to save his life. Apparently, he had made a deal with the devil. After being delivered, he lost his job because he could no longer compete well. There's always a cost to following Jesus. We should thank God for smashing our idols. They get in the way of fixing our eyes on the true Lord.

Even in the less severe case of oppression, the "pin down"—as I have coined it—is most common. Someone feels like they cannot stand up out of bed, as if something very heavy is weighing down all four of their limbs or putting severe pressure on their chest, keeping them down. Disturbing cases of sexual violation by an evil entity have even been documented.

In cases where heavy occult practice is prevalent, levitation of objects and people is normal. Items may fly off the walls or slide off tables. The vomiting of objects can occur during an exorcism. One woman from whom I had exorcised multiple demons would run to the toilet to vomit out a strange fluid after each deliverance.

In one recorded case of demon possession in 1928, the demoniac clung to the wall like a spider, while the nuns had difficulty bringing her back to the mattress.[6] This poor Iowa girl had been cursed by her despicable and unchaste father, who offered her to the devil after she refused to commit incest with him. She, as well, vomited buckets of strange substances daily, even though she barely ate anything during the twenty-three-day exorcism.[7] Some stomach fluids were habitually spat from a body that had become so discolored and disfigured through unusual bloating that its regular contours were unrecognizable. This peculiar fluctuation of body weight even resulted in the permanent bending of the metal bed frame.[8]

Other exorcists record the manifestation of burns and bruising on the patient, the smell of strange sulfuric odors, the presence of multiple voices, unusual behavior from house pets, and a range of unimaginable and frightening manifestations.[9] Supernatural occurrences accompanying demon possession aren't uncommon, which is why the Roman Ritual of 1618 includes the following clues as confirming signs in diagnosis:

The ability to communicate with some facility in a strange or foreign tongue (such as Latin).
The faculty to divulge future and hidden events.
The capacity to display powers that are beyond the subject's age and natural condition.[10]

Seventeenth-century orthodox Lutheran theologian Johannes Andreas Quenstedt also listed monstrosity in

6. Carl Vogl, *Begone, Satan! A Soul-Stirring Account of Diabolical Possession in Iowa*, trans. Celestine Kapsner (Tan Books and Publishers, 1973), 13.
7. Vogl, *Begone, Satan!*, 19.
8. Vogl, *Begone, Satan!*, 21.
9. Amorth, *An Exorcist Tells His Story*, 124.
10. Philip T. Weller, ed. and trans., *The Roman Ritual* (Bruce Publishing Co., 1964), 217.

gestures, obscenity in speech, the capability to voice exact reproductions of animal noises without the disposition of the required organs, clairvoyance, and self-hatred.[11]

Alien Abduction

Alleged accounts of alien abduction should not be impetuously dismissed. One man whom I highly respect had a sister who claimed abduction in a cornfield. The details of the physical abuse she underwent were uncanny. She was a totally normal and sane woman, but this event entirely changed and ruined her life. No one believed her story. The worst challenge, as is the case with demonism, is disbelief from others in whom you confide.

I've found that to be true in my own life, which led me to write my first book after many years of reluctance. I did it so that others could be consoled by the fact that they weren't crazy. Why are people so hesitant to believe in physical encounters with the devil? Firstly, they aren't generally scientific, otherwise people would follow the scientific process of analysis and not simply dismiss a hypothesis that doesn't jibe with their preconceived notions and beliefs. They're unconsciously afraid of suffering cognitive dissonance. God pokes a hole into their non-Christian worldviews, which are inadequate for explaining their own observations of the world.

Secondly, they're often terrified of the life implications if they admit that such monsters are real and not fiction. If aliens exist and are a kind of embodied demonic entity, people have a lot to fear, and any sensible person would be

11. As quoted in Robert H. Bennett, *I Am Not Afraid* (Concordia Publishing House, 2014), 150.

compelled to at the very least consider surrendering their life to Jesus. But they don't want to give up their lives to God. Even we Christians, as sinners, want to maintain control.

Strange and Beastly Behavior

Other less supernatural signs of possession include the deformation of movements, such as inhuman revelry, facial contortion, immodest laughter, spitting, removing clothes, lacerating oneself (Mark 9:20; Luke 8:27), and ferocious growls.

Animal behavior is particularly noteworthy, as it involves corrupting reason in a person and turning them into a subhuman beast. God made humans distinct from animals. In the 1990s, some charismatic groups claimed the Holy Spirit was manifesting Himself in Christians by taking the form of animals.[12] During worship, Christians would behave like chickens, dogs, and cows. I remember reading about one of the pastors involved who admitted that it wasn't clear to him how to decipher whether he was witnessing the presence of the Holy Spirit or demons due to the similarity in these spiritual signs.

Such activity is clearly demonic. When I was an inner-city pastor, I was once subjected to a growling voice on a phone in a cold call from a deeply disturbed drug addict. I rushed to the house to find the demoniac crouched on a chair in the posture of a rabid dog. The difference between human and animal is a God-given soul, which includes rationality and reason. Accordingly, we are stewards of bodies that have been entrusted to our care. "Our" bodies are not really ours. They

12. Wikipedia, "Toronto Blessing," accessed November 7, 2024, https://en.wikipedia.org/wiki/Toronto_Blessing.

belong to God. We are expected to behave in ways befitting our status as the crown of God's creation and creatures made in the image of the Creator.

Instead, demons seek to be what they are not. They want us to do the same. One reason drunkenness and drug abuse are sinful is because of their impact on human reason.[13] "Drunkenness in the spirit" is a mockery of the redeemed bodies, minds, and souls of Christians.[14] God expects us to be sober (1 Thess. 5:6).

Ironically, while animals always behave in a natural way, humankind does not, though we are naturally superior. Incest and other sexual perversions have no serious parallels in the natural world (Jude 7). Yet the devil finds clever ways of twisting human reason to justify such activities. We betray ourselves as more perverse than beasts. The demons are quite content to behave in perverted ways as is fitting to their rebellious manner and, therefore, use humans as puppets in those games. The enemy desires us to lose our self-control and govern our lives by the feelings of our sinful hearts.

A less dramatic and much more common sign of demonic oppression is the observance of diluted and dark pupils that just seem off somehow. Again, the eyes are the window of the soul (see Prov. 30:17; Matt. 6:22–23). Christians shouldn't make theological decisions based on their feelings or experiences, but when other demonic symptoms are present, the eyes can be a helpful check in confirming one's suspicions.

Horrible shouting (Mark 5:5) or unusual periods of silence are also symptoms. You may find yourself speaking directly to a suspect and having them behave as if they aren't

13. It's also sinful since it deprives us of our chance to help our neighbors. When we are intoxicated, we are not in a position to assist others in need.

14. The Lord wishes that we *overdrink* and *overeat* at the water and food of His Word, making us "drunk" in the Spirit spiritually, not literally.

listening to you or are listening to someone else. I have even been hushed by an occult practitioner under the influence of the devil. He accused me, midsentence, of interrupting another voice. He tilted his ear away from me and nodded as he received some kind of instruction from an entity invisible and inaudible to me.

I can't count the number of times that a demonically oppressed individual has told me they're not to listen to me. Sometimes those under demonic oppression have confessed that they had seen me in their dreams, even before meeting me for the first time, and were told to stay away. One man said he was on his way to visit me and almost turned his car around since the voice was so strong and persuasive. I attribute this not to myself but to my office as a faithful pastor whom the demons know will prayerfully rebuke them with the Word of God. The same voice told that man to kill himself weeks later. Thanks be to God, the Holy Spirit intervened.

One man who was demonically oppressed would fall asleep midsentence whenever religion came up in conversation. Another man whom I was instructing in the Christian Faith but who had dabbled in the satanic arts for many years would plug his ears and tuck his head between his knees in an effort to block out the sound of my probing questions.

Appearance of Curses

Sometimes there's a general appearance of those under demonic influence as being cursed in key areas of life. They just appear to be "unlucky" and nothing seems to go right with them.

Yet again, one needs to be very careful with judgments here. Remember Job, who appeared more cursed than any

117

other living creature, even though that wasn't the case at all. He was a type of the Suffering Servant, Jesus, the Crucified One, who remains the most blessed of all people. Christians must never judge the presence or absence of God based on experiences, feelings, or emotions, which can easily mislead us. God's promises, on the other hand, are solid. So the speculation of cursing should only be considered an indicator if other symptoms are already present.

The fact that demoniacs are usually worse off in life can become a convenient and persuasive argument for those who aren't fully willing to throw the evil one out of their lives because they're falsely convinced that demons are philanthropic helpers. But again, be careful. You don't want people following Jesus because they want an easier life. Jesus doesn't promise that, as we make our way through the narrow gate. "For the gate is wide and the way is easy that leads to destruction, and those who enter by it are many. For the gate is narrow and the way is hard that leads to life, and those who find it are few" (Matt. 7:13–14). To be sure, Jesus promises to never leave us or forsake us (Heb. 13:5–6) in our journey, but unity with Christ comes with crosses, so that we can "rejoice in our sufferings, knowing that suffering produces endurance, and endurance produces character, and character produces hope, and hope does not put us to shame, because God's love has been poured into our hearts through the Holy Spirit who has been given to us" (Rom. 5:3–5).

A Roman Catholic friend of mine was mystified by a series of bizarre events that had transpired over a two-month period. Then he discovered a curse had been placed upon him by a woman who had gripes with the Church and dabbled in witchcraft. The curse was easily broken through prayer.

Part and parcel with suspected curses as a common sign of demonic influence is that the affected person seems to not be the same as before. Many parents deal with teenagers who are naturally moody and go through lengthy periods of social withdrawal. But a Christian parent who is emotionally connected with their child knows the difference between the normal challenges of adolescence and when something else is at work. I know of one parent who discovered that her lonely child had tapped into a perverted internet community during the pandemic lockdowns. After a few weeks, she slowly began to turn into a different version of herself. At first, she withdrew to her bedroom for hours, obsessed with being online. She started to skip most meals and refused to speak to her parents except through screams with vulgar language. Then she refused to attend church. Finally, she denied the Christian Faith.

Yet praise God, she was delivered. After recovery, she admitted that it was as if some creature had taken over her capacity to make clear decisions and speak in normal ways. She couldn't recall many of her rebellious and violent acts. This, too, is a typical sign: blackouts, falling into zombielike trances, and forgetfulness of things done.

Hatred of Holy Things

The aversion to holy things like the Bible, crucifixes, religious images, and Christian tracts and brochures is a common symptom of both severe oppression and possession. The inability to pray and speak the holy name of Jesus and Christian creeds is a clear giveaway that demons are active. At the same time, some demons will tolerate these things despite their natural discomfort with anything involving the Church. They want to trick the Christian helper into believing that "there is nothing to see here."

But the more deeply you pry, speaking not only in general terms of a good and loving God but specifically declaring the works of the Lord Jesus Christ through His salutary acts, the less tolerable the demon will find the conversation, and the kinds of blatant physical reactions and their escalation will determine the degree of evil presence.

Whenever I suspect a demonic presence, I subtly use the name of Jesus as often as I can in conversation, incorporating various descriptions of His holy ministry of deliverance. I say the name slowly, enunciating each syllable, all the while monitoring for uncomfortable behavior in the person, as evidenced by facial expression and eye motion. Sometimes I will ask them to repeat a prayer after me or with me, in which I observe them with one eye open. Difficulty in even mentioning Jesus is a sign. Some will only partially be able to utter that word. The name of Jesus the Christ is the most powerful word in the universe—and the devil knows it.

Less Severe Symptoms

There's a plethora of other less severe signs, but we should be careful basing a diagnosis upon them. Habitual jeering at others, filthy talk, and foul language are sinful, but they aren't necessarily displays of demonism. But when other more critical symptoms are evident, these can definitely be additional indicators. It's important to carefully observe for these behaviors repeated in those who have been delivered and are recovering.

Overcaution should be encouraged, for when such "mild" signs reappear, they can be indicative of a larger problem of demons reentering. The most serious mild symptom is spiritual and mental depression. The devil targets those he believes he can still dupe in his pursuit of regaining lost territory. So attempted suicide (Mark 9:22) or suicidal temptations among those struggling with demonism are very common, as death is the ultimate goal of the devil. Self-mutilation and "gender reassignment" surgeries, appallingly popular among Generation Alpha, are attacks on God's beautiful creation and a subtle display of self-hatred. Suicide is its logical conclusion.

Mental illness isn't necessarily directly demonic, but Christians should never underestimate the role of the devil in the playground of our minds in their fallen state. All brokenness in the human experience is a result of sin and the devil. And with approximately one-quarter of US adults struggling with some kind of mental health issue[15]—and many relying solely on pharmaceuticals and secular counseling for help—I believe there's more demonic activity going on in our society today than a generation ago.

Making Sense of Symptoms

When attempting to assess the degree of demonization, much caution must be taken in final judgments. All circumstances and symptoms must be taken into consideration case by case when proceeding with an exorcism. Most importantly, whenever possible, no Christian should tackle these issues alone.

In light of the wide scale of potential symptoms of oppression or possession, how does one responsibly determine the degree of demonic presence in a suspected victim? How do we know whether an acquaintance is just having a bad day or is actually under the deep influence of dark, evil forces? A false or sloppy diagnosis can be a pretty embarrassing affair, never mind a perilous one. Jumping the gun is sure

15. NIH, "Mental Illness," National Institute of Mental Health, accessed December 19, 2024, https://www.nimh.nih.gov/health/statistics/mental-illness.

to jeopardize friendships, relationships, and reputations of many stakeholders. It can even land you in court. How to decipher demonic presence is the next "need to know" before proceeding with—in the rare and worst-case scenario—an actual exorcism.

6

DETERMINING AND RESPONDING TO DEMONIC PRESENCE

The key strategy in determining to what degree, if any, a demonic entity is present in a suspected demoniac is simply gathering information by asking questions. The goal here is to decipher whether the suspect has been dabbling in false religion, especially the occult, or has participated in any sins of a sexual nature. Because the misuse of both legal and illegal drugs can be an entry point for demons, knowledge of medical history, especially when it comes to mental health, can be of great help.

My system involves asking simple and direct questions pertaining to a suspect's lifestyle. I ask a series of both closed- and open-ended questions, such as "Do you consider yourself a practicing Christian, and if so, can you tell me about what that means to you? Are you baptized? When and where did that happen? What does it mean to you?" Now, not every baptism is legitimate, even if the individual thinks it is. The validity and efficacy of baptism is not based on a subjective experience but on the Word of God and the authority of His Church. For example, the exact words of Matthew 28:19 must be used and the baptism must be done "in the name of the Father and of the Son and of the Holy Spirit." Months after working with one demoniac, I discovered she had been "baptized" in a bathtub by her mother, who wanted nothing to do with the Church or organized religion, but wanted "it done" just to be safe. Only God knows what words were used. God has no patience for abuse of His sacraments. His Word is majestic and mighty, but it's not magic. When faith is absent, you've got a problem. Often, though, this can be dealt with through deliberate biblical instruction and Christian catechesis, which is the Holy Spirit's way of creating and strengthening faith.

Other questions include: "Do you take drugs, and if so what kind and why? What are your thoughts about fornication and homosexuality? What do you like to do for fun, and are any of those hobbies occult-based or something God may have a problem with?" I then try to direct the discussion into a deeper description of their spiritual life by examining the degree to which they believe they have broken the Ten Commandments. I walk with them through each one of these ten "diagnostic tools," seeking to unveil any recurring themes and paying special attention to any deliberate acts of sacrilege or rebellion against God, any involvement with rituals associated with the occult or idol worship or anti-Christian cults, any use of hallucinogenic or other drugs that rob a person of self-control, any occasions of sexual defilement, any signs of violence, and any occasion when God's means of grace have been rejected or defiled. Non-verbal language can become as important as oral responses if, in fact, a demonic entity is present.[1] Accordingly, I carefully observe body language and eye movements, and I am attentive to any awkwardness regarding certain topics or abnormal reactions to any sacred phraseology. There is a direct correlation between the degree to which demonism is present and an individual's outward control over his or her life. So even at this questioning phase, in extreme cases, the person may not be able to say, or may react strangely to the utterance of, biblical words and concepts such as the Lord's Prayer, various names for our Savior, and Christian creeds.

If I'm in my office, I always have a crucifix hung somewhere clearly visible. An empty cross is better than nothing, but it's not as powerful or useful a tool as one affixed with an image of the crucified Christ (1 Cor. 1:23). An empty cross can simply be a symbol of the death penalty. The devil doesn't fear it. But a corpus on the cross is a symbol of the sacrificial atonement of the only Son of God achieving the salvation of the world and the destruction of the kingdom of darkness. It shows "the God of peace [who crushes] Satan under [our] feet" (Rom. 16:20). It's no wonder Satan hates that image.

I also wear a cross around my neck 24/7, and when counseling, I normally have it in plain sight. After years of experience, I have discovered that I can decipher much about someone's spiritual state by the way he or she reacts to that image. Complete avoidance after even a glance is a bad sign. After all, Jesus is the Word made visible, "the image of the invisible God" (Col. 1:15). God's Word penetrates the heart not only through the ears but also through the eyes. I've witnessed responses ranging from hardened, bitter anger to teary-eyed softness from those in a state of spiritual or

---

1. Lutheran Church of Australia (LCA), "Spiritual Oppression" in *Rites and Resources for Pastoral Care* (Openbook, 1998), 140.

mental crisis when I point or refer to that cross upon which hangs humankind's selfless Redeemer and Lord.

I never leave home without my cross; I never know when I might need it. I've been caught off guard more times than I can recount in this line of work. Once a young girl began to slap my body like a broken robot on high speed when I proclaimed to her the love of God in Christ. Even though it hurt, I chose to just let myself be her punching bag for about one full minute. She finally just broke down weeping. Evil was defeated by love. The devil can't stand true acts of love: "Do not be overcome by evil, but overcome evil with good" (Rom. 12:21). Sometimes, the greatest acts of love involve not only the tolerance but even the embracement of evil. Our Lord says: "But I say to you, don't resist the one who is evil" (Matt. 5:39). If someone strikes us and we don't bite back, the world and the devil call us cowards but our Lord commends us. His opinion matters most.

When dealing with someone who is obviously under deep demonic influence (such as a case of oppression bordering on possession), you'll usually notice something is wrong with the person the moment you start speaking about our Triune God. Without minimizing the importance of assessments conducted by Christian mental health professionals or medical doctors,[2] when interviewing the individual, you must be careful to be guided by God's Word rather than psychology and secular thinking patterns.

This filtering process is less awkward for a pastor, because people are accustomed to sharing their problems with clergy and aren't as adverse or surprised when we poke around in

---

2. In South and Central America, where Roman Catholicism maintains a cultural stronghold in the daily lives of people, the clergy are often the first point of contact for all concerns, both medical and spiritual. The opposite is true in highly secularized places such as North America.

their private lives. A pastor's office or church is essentially a clinical environment for spiritual patients.

For those who have had little connection to the Church, the deciphering process needs to be handled differently and more carefully—employing interrogative questions in a more subtle manner. I never send anyone away, even when they are totally ignorant about Christianity and seem utterly lost and without hope. God puts people in our lives, and we are asked to meet with them in their hurts, pains, and challenges. In light of the unfortunate fact that there are so many pastors who are uncomfortable with or skeptical of this topic and area of ministry, shepherding by an ill-equipped layperson may be all a precious lamb lost to demonism will ever receive.

Treatments Vary

Depending on the degree of demonization, treatment will vary. Even the categories of oppression versus possession are not absolute but rather intended to help explain phenomena instead of pigeonhole individuals. To discredit the eccentricities of personal stories and complex histories is not only disrespectful but unhelpful. All solutions are tailor-made when we understand that each person has a unique set of problems and sins. That's why individual confession and absolution offered by pastors are so important for all Christians, since forgiveness of sins usually pertains to specific things that are wrong with us and involve pastoral care and advice. So don't be a legalist or a kind of Christian witch doctor, thinking that just because something worked in one case, it can be applied to all. Even using a rite for deliverance and exorcism—as I outline below—provides only one of many flexible tools within the larger framework of deliverance ministry.

In cases of minor demonic influence or weak oppression, you may witness victims just wrestling with basic crises of conscience or issues of spiritual anxiety. For example, they may be burdened with a loss of assurance that God loves them, that their salvation is secure in Christ, or that they have a meaningful purpose in life.

When I was a missionary in Africa, I met with two Christian men who had just had a fistfight. Afterward, both were repentant, but one man could not forgive himself. He lay on his bed with his face hidden in his mattress. When I proclaimed to him that his sins were forgiven, he began to violently punch himself in the head. It was as if someone else had taken control of his fists. He obviously had deeper issues than a mere confrontation with a coworker. I laid my hand on him, prayed, and repeated the message that Jesus loved him and that His death took away all his sins. The man finally broke down weeping. He relaxed, praised God, and latched on to me with a hug.

Often, those delivered from possession are tempted to believe they are worthless, and they wonder if God really does accept them and forgive them for their bad choices. This leads to despair: "God doesn't want me. God can't help me." Whether you judge it as a legitimate emotion matters little. It's a real feeling that the devil uses for his destructive ends. Only Jesus can release a sinner from the chains of guilt and self-pity. Jesus says, "The thief comes only to steal and kill and destroy. I came that they may have life and have it abundantly" (John 10:10).

In the case where you find a person obsessed by an evil desire and having essentially lost all emotional control, such as with addiction, the prevalent thought is *I am a failure. I can't change. I can't help myself.* Believe it or not, suicide is often a "solution" taken by those who don't actually want to end their lives. They just want the pain to stop: the heartbreak, the depression, the trauma, the hopelessness.

But there is always something a victim can do to take back control of his or her life. For example, someone addicted to pornography can choose not to drive to stores that sell dirty magazines and videos or can block websites by changing the parameters on their internet browser. To succumb to perpetual temptation toward certain sins without displaying any tangible signs of repentance will certainly lead to further oppression and even possession. "Whoever makes a practice of sinning is of the devil, for the devil has been sinning from the beginning. The reason the Son of God appeared was to destroy the works of the devil" (1 John 3:8). Deliverance for addicts happens through the deliberate and pointed application of God's law and gospel that leads to sincere confession of sin, prayer, and joyful absolution. They need to know that they will only find true freedom by entrusting their burdens and illness into the strong and compassionate arms of Jesus Christ.

Sometimes, in cases of abuse, the victim may be entirely innocent. Yet still, he or she needs to confess the shame suffered in order to deal with any guilt, resentment, fear, hatred, and the like, however unsubstantiated these feelings may be. In the horrific case of rape or child abuse, for example, an innocent person may feel guilty by no fault of their own. Whatever feelings the victim has—such as guilt due to their sins or shame due to the sins done against them—they need to be acknowledged and not denied. The bottom-line solution to peace with God and within is taking everything ugly that clings to you, in spite of who is responsible—both a broken spirit and a contrite heart—and offer it to Jesus (Ps. 51:17), who takes it all away.

Confessing to pastors, priests, other Christians, and directly to God all amount to tossing one's brokenness at the foot of Christ's cross and letting Him deal with it. And, unlike garbage trucks that only pick up trash that is carefully sorted into different specialized bins, Jesus doesn't mind taking the one big bag and dealing with it Himself. "Here You go, Jesus. You asked for it." He can cope with the disgusting content as He has proven at Calvary. It's a two-step process.

Firstly, we need to admit we are carrying this ugly mound of spiritual filth: "Take no part in the unfruitful works of darkness, but instead expose them" (Eph. 5:11). Secondly, we need to boldly cast our load onto Christ, who has "cast all our sins into the depths of the sea" (Mic. 7:19), "because he cares for [us]" (1 Pet. 5:7).

Again, sometimes we are part of "unfruitful work" not by any choice of our own. There are Christians who've been possessed due to curses and witchcraft done to them—and by the way, "white" witchcraft is just as bad as "black"; it's just more covert. But by exposing it all, we give it to our Lord who "has delivered us from the domain of darkness and transferred us to the kingdom of his beloved Son, in whom we have redemption, the forgiveness of sins" (Col. 1:13–14). Although we remain sinners affected by the darkness of sin and the devil simply by virtue of being fallen humans making our way in a fallen world in our journey toward a certain death, we are also pilgrims clothed with the righteousness of Jesus, rejoicing in the promise of a new heavenly home. "For the wages of sin is death, but the free gift of God is eternal life in Christ Jesus our Lord" (Rom. 6:23).

Though being a sinner/saint is a paradox, it's enlightening. It's the only way of explaining why we holy children of God still behave in unholy and rebellious ways. We remain sinners but are forgiven all by the grace of God and the blood of Christ through faith alone.

Question 1: To What Degree Do You Identify as Being Christian?

Ultimately then, in prodding into the private life of a possible hostage of the evil one, firstly, you are trying to measure to what extent the person understands what it means to live as a helpless yet loved sinner, saved and cleansed by Christ. To what degree do they identify as being Christian and believe the Good News to be true? Holy baptism is our transfer out of the kingdom of darkness to the kingdom of light (Col. 1:13), so finding out whether they have been baptized in the name of the Father, Son, and Holy Spirit, and asking whether they treasure all that the Lord has given them through that sacrament, is a good place to start. Do they believe they have been fully washed by the blood of Jesus? Why or why not?

In Bible times, the idea of "unclean" didn't just involve moral filth but indicated a more profound theological point regarding our status before our holy Creator: We are separated from God due to our very nature and status as sinners who are born enemies of His kingdom. So unclean foods in the Old Testament were not just *morally* unacceptable but made God's people *ritually* impure. They blocked the relationship between God and humanity that He had established through His system of worship. Those who deliberately ate unclean foods defiled the space in which people and God related and exposed an alliance with false religion and false gods.

Children tracking insect-infested mud from the outside onto the clean carpet of the family dining room are rightfully scolded. The filth contaminates the living space for both host and guest. This is how it works within the kingdom of God. There are conditions to entry. Jesus's cleansing of us spiritually means He adopts us into His perfect and holy household. Yet there are still conditions upon admittance, and there remain fitting and unfitting ways of living there. And those who don't appreciate the rules, and the reason for them, may find themselves back on the dirty streets.

In the parable of the wedding banquet, the improperly dressed guest was cast into outer darkness because he had refused to clothe himself with the garment to which he would have easily had access (Matt. 22:1–14). This rude guest chose to insult the host. Christ's robe of righteousness goes hand in hand with His invitation to join Him in His kingdom. Both already belong to us. Yet the question remains: Do we treasure His invaluable, gracious gift, or do we rudely treat it as a filthy rag?

We are saved through faith alone, yet we are still expected to live a lifestyle worthy of our name as citizens of His glorious country and inhabitants of His heavenly home (Phil. 3:20). Through repentance, we live as children of light and not of darkness. "The night is far gone; the day is at hand. So then let us cast off the works of darkness and put on the armor of light" (Rom. 13:12) because "[we] who once were alienated and hostile in mind, doing evil deeds, he has now reconciled in his body of flesh by his death, in order to present [us] holy and blameless and above reproach before him" (Col. 1:21–22).

In the early church, when baptism and reception into Holy Communion were the result of a lengthy period of instruction for adults, converts from paganism were required to demonstrate the sincerity of their faith by living a Christian lifestyle. "Bear fruits in keeping with repentance" (Luke 3:8). Christianity can't be reduced to an intellectual adherence to certain doctrines without serious consideration of a change of behavior. We have been made righteous by the blood of Jesus, by grace. We are temples of the Holy Spirit. Neither unrepentant sin nor unclean spirits belong in this holy house. Possession of Christians is thus rare.

Yet if we're honest, we must admit that we share this temple with the evil one throughout our lives. The story of the prodigal son is a daily experience for us sinner/saints. Even though we are the son, we drift away from faith and live like foolish pigs in our acts and attitudes, "like a dog that returns to his vomit" (Prov. 26:11). Thanks be to God that He remains the Lord of the temple and refuses to cast us away from His presence when we allow Him to cleanse our hearts through the continual forgiveness of our sins. But we still need to repent.

An alcoholic lamenting his or her addiction while hanging around in a liquor store can be pitied but not taken seriously. The ministry of deliverance involves removal of impurity of all kinds as our holy and righteous Lord takes His rightful place in the hearts of His creatures. But the devil loves to dig up dirt in those houses to make us think they're an unsuitable habitation for our Lord. He brings back what has long been forgiven and gets us to doubt the victorious work of Christ.

He does this with all of us, but especially the oppressed and possessed. One man I was counseling hid himself in a hotel in a state of emergency. He begged me to visit him as soon as possible. I thought he was suicidal. I raced to his room and knocked on the door. I said, "What's the matter?" He said, "I just need someone to tell me that God loves me and forgives me for all my crap." For him, these words couldn't wait. If a tweet in the hands of a politician is more dangerous than a bullet in a soldier's rifle, imagine the spiritual significance of a divine word on our souls. Everything for this man depended upon hearing a very simple message. At the end of the day, forgiveness of sins is the secret ingredient to the ministry of deliverance.

Question 2: To What Degree Do You Want Deliverance?

The next question deciphers the degree to which the person is willing to entrust themselves to Jesus in both word and deed. Most people want freedom from the devil, but they don't want to become a servant of Jesus. Again, part of this process is not just confessing an orthodox faith. Are they willing to change their lives in a way that aligns with their Christian confession, such as giving up evil items and practices, cutting ties with certain groups of friends, quitting morally questionable jobs, or changing living situations that invite temptation? These are all good questions.

However, sometimes what is sin to one person may not be sin to another (Rom. 14:22–23). I try to determine what is most important to the individual in an effort to reveal to him or her specific false gods, since a "god," after all, can be defined as the thing in which you place most of your trust and without which you cannot live. False gods are always personal in this sense. One man I knew swore he would never drink a bottle of wine with any images of the devil on the label, even cute and silly ones of pointed tails and horns. They would trigger bad memories. But he didn't have a problem with his collection of rock music record covers, which I thought were way worse. I personally would have been fine with the first but not the second. The freedom we have in Christ allows for wiggle room when it comes to these kinds of choices. An idol for one is not necessarily an idol for another. So I find it helpful to describe a healthy Christian life so that they can better see the ways in which

134

their lives do not harmonize with what the one true God intends for them.

If the oppressed show major resistance, and there is basically no sincere interest in breaking bondage, perhaps they need to suffer longer with their chains before they come to their senses. When someone hoards their sins and lives selfishly, spurning all that has been purchased and won by our Lord's atoning sacrifice on the cross, we have no choice but to "deliver this man to Satan for the destruction of the flesh, so that his spirit may be saved in the day of the Lord" (1 Cor. 5:5). They have excommunicated themselves from God's love. Availing some space to reconsider their bad choices is the only honest decision a Christian caregiver can make. I have made the mistake of attempting to live the life of such people for them, desiring deliverance more than they. Not only does this make me susceptible to burnout but chances are, afterward, the demons return and with a fury anyway.

We shouldn't be ashamed that we are "the aroma of Christ to God among those who are being saved and among those who are perishing, to one a fragrance from death to death, to the other a fragrance from life to life" (2 Cor. 2:15–16). The Church doesn't promote conversions through arm twisting. We aren't salespeople. We are truth-tellers, and if anyone is too self-confident, stupid, or gutless to grasp hold of the greatest of gifts when it's handed to them on a silver platter, they only have themselves to blame for the aftermath.

I've often been too eager to provide pastoral care to people who ultimately care less about their freedom than I do. Like those who break it off with a toxic partner only to find themselves running back to them a few days later, they say they want liberty but actually yearn for slavery. Like a pig that returns to wallow in the muck after being washed (2 Pet. 2:22), they return to the poisonous and destructive relationship knowing full well it's destined to end badly. Their body has become too comfortable with the darkness, though their soul craves the light. They are afraid and doubtful that a better life awaits. They lack faith. Fear of hell doesn't equal a love of heaven. So some choose to stay within their prison cell though the door has been swung open. Their last state becomes worse than their first (Luke 11:26).

True repentance involves sincere confession of a miserable state. Only the Holy Spirit can stir up such hearts. In such cases, Christian helpers need to be patient, take a step back, and simply pray that the victim takes a firm stand against the enemy by resolutely showing the impostor the door—and for good. Those who undertake the ministry of deliverance need to remember Christ's warning about the danger of an evil spirit returning to an empty house with seven other spirits even worse than itself (Matt. 12:43–45; Luke 11:24–26). Therefore, we need to take on the battle warily and without too much haste.

No Christian can do the believing for another Christian. If someone wants others to fight their battles for them, they won't succeed. They themselves need to allow the angels to valiantly combat the enemy while clinging to their own God-given armor. We all need to carry our crosses together. But a balanced lift means we don't shift the weight from one person's side entirely onto the other. And because Jesus carries all our crosses on our behalf, an individual who won't own their issues is essentially depriving their Lord of the opportunity to save them. You can't help such a person other than to pray for them and rebuke them with the divine Word.

One nominally Catholic man from whom I had cast some demons was very grateful for my service. Now he could sleep better. He felt more at peace. As was my custom, I counseled him to recommence a life of prayer and deeper devotion,

Bible study, church attendance, and participation in the worship life of a local Christian community. However, he didn't think he was ready for any of that.

So the second time he visited me to ask for deliverance from demonic entities, I didn't do it. It was a painful pastoral decision. He wanted me to pray for him and to rebuke the devil again on his behalf, but he wasn't willing to do any of it himself. He wouldn't own his problem and take responsibility for his spiritual state. And, so, the demons remained.

I didn't sleep well that night, my unrest due to my own lack of faith. It turned out that the demoniac didn't sleep either, since he called me a couple of days later confessing that he had just endured some of the worst days of his life. I didn't ask what he meant. He didn't want to offer details either. It didn't matter. He begged to see me again, unequivocally insisting, "I am ready now."

He was ready to say no to the devil; ready to face—to *own*—his problem. Yet I still made him wait a bit. I had him make the plans, set the appointment, and choose the location. Then, together, he and I organized a meeting at a local church for a second exorcism.

Hidden Blessings in Failure

In my experience, despite trying to do everything right, in many cases the demons return. Just like a recovering alcoholic will have a terrible time resisting the temptation to drink at the beginning of his or her new journey, there will be slipups now and again for recovering demoniacs. Some interpret repeat exorcisms on the same person as failure. Yet in my opinion, success isn't measured by whether the person still encounters demonic attacks but whether they return to

Christ and stay there. And even though society seeks quick fixes, God's timeline is usually different from ours.

Of course, prayers of repentance and appeals that the Holy Spirit fill the person's heart and control their life follow each time. But even when the outcomes are lamentable, each visit represents another occasion to pray. After all, had I not been called to help out with whatever the situation, I wouldn't have prayed at that moment. I would've gone about my day thinking only about myself. I wouldn't have had the opportunity to rejoice with "the angels of God over one sinner who repents" (Luke 15:10).

All suffering is a blessing in disguise when it directs our attention to God in heaven and to His grace, teaching us to rely on God's mercy more and more. I would rather a recovering demoniac struggle their whole life with demons and remain connected to Christ and His Church than an ex-demoniac live a happy, unperturbed life post-exorcism and forget their constant reliance on our Savior, letting their relationship with the Lord erode. I suppose this is why "blessed are the poor in spirit, for theirs is the kingdom of heaven" (Matt. 5:3).

A nineteenth-century German exorcist, Johann Blumhardt, describes his experiences of casting thousands of demons out of a young girl who had suffered from occult rituals performed on her by her uncle. After years of suffering, she was finally delivered from the devil.[3] Blumhardt shares how he couldn't make sense of the failure to keep her free, until many years later when she allegedly ended up working with mentally challenged children. She was one of the few caregivers who could relate to the personal loneliness and

---

3. See Dieter Ising, *Johann Christoph Blumhardt, Life and Work: A New Biography*, trans. Monty Ledford (Cascade Books, 2009).

isolation those children suffered. She became a lovely tool of the Holy Spirit in healing their lives. Who would've thought such ugliness could be the cause of such beauty?

Question 3: Are You Ready to Honestly Confess Your Sins?

The final cluster of questions is intended to pinpoint a personalized cure and offer pastoral and Christian care by deciphering whether the demonic influence can be explained as a general, ordinary attack or the extraordinary kind of oppression or possession. Applying the forgiveness of sins is a tailor-made affair. To just tell people that they are forgiven in general terms doesn't necessarily fix the individual sin for which they truly feel guilty.

That is why the ancient practice of confession and absolution (John 20:22–23), when done responsibly, can be such an effective mode of healing. Facilitated by the pastor, the confessor gets one-on-one time with Jesus as the Word governs the conversation. When it comes to spirituality, if sin is the world's problem, the answer is the forgiveness of sins. "For I will be merciful toward their iniquities, and I will remember their sins no more" (Heb. 8:12).

Guiding someone who is oppressed through acknowledging sins so that they can be exposed and eliminated can be likened to an exterminator searching for cockroaches in the house in order to poison them. Once they are identified and confessed, they can be destroyed "in the name of the Father, and of the Son, and of the Holy Spirit." Pastors have an advantage doing this, since they are trained to ask suitable and targeted questions in order to pry into those dark and secret places in search of foul nests of evil critters. Clergy are also under the "confessional seal" guaranteeing confidentiality. This makes people more apt to confide in them

139

versus fellow Christians. Even if this was the only reason, pastors should always be a major participant in the ministry of deliverance.

Telling your sins privately and individually to a spiritually mature Christian—or in private confession with a skilled and experienced pastor—offers invaluable help to spiritual freedom. When the pastor is courageous and bold enough to ask the tough questions and lead you to identify these dark areas of your life, then the Holy Spirit is actively at work exposing every one of your "fruitless deeds of darkness" so that "everything that is illuminated" becomes visible (Eph. 5:11, 13 NIV). Every idolized aspiration, misplaced love, or deranged thought is dealt with by the grace of God. "So it is said: 'Wake up, sleeper, rise from the dead, and Christ will shine on you'" (v. 14 NIV). Like a dentist poking at each single tooth looking for a cavity, the Lord uses His pastors as a probe within souls. When you actively put yourself under a shepherd's scrutiny, regularly submitting yourself to this process of exposing what you would rather keep concealed, you are keeping the devil at arm's length. "For when I kept silent, my bones wasted away" (Ps. 32:3). When you confess your sins, you "resist the devil" (James 4:7) and he flees from you.

In the classic novel *Crime and Punishment*, Fyodor Dosto-evsky skillfully ties together the spiritual and psychological dimensions of human experience. The story tells of a man who murders another man. Subsequently, the murderer's whole life is shaped by the belief that everybody knows about his crime—even though nobody suspects in the least that he did it. Years later, the murderer gives himself up to the police because he thinks they are about to arrest him, not due to penitential guilt but because of the distress and agony caused by his internalized obsession. The police are thrilled to have finally closed the case after so many years. They never had an inkling who the killer was.

The protagonist was under the illusion that he was being targeted by the authorities because the lens through which he filtered reality was skewed. That's how sin works in our hearts. When it is unresolved, it overtakes us. Yet unlike Dostoevsky's character, our angst isn't demonstrated in paranoia or a nervous breakdown but in the subtleties of our behaviors and attitudes.

Overall, by asking tough questions, the practitioner tries to discern the degree of demonic influence by determining the demonic entry points so that they can be closed. Points of attack and roots to how the demonism began and continues to influence are sought out. Objects and experiences are not the only portals. The chains of a wide range of negative emotions, such as resentment, shame, and guilt, from which a victim cannot seem to be set free can only be unlocked by the key of the gospel (John 20:23). All this is important for prevention so that the critters don't return (Matt. 12:43–45). The discovery of these causes, symptoms, and effects will prove greatly advantageous in providing effective aftercare. For all these reasons, the ministry of deliverance is part of wider pastoral ministry involving Christian relationships through caregivers, pastors, and mature lay Christians.

The Unholy Trinity of Drugs, Sex, and False Religion

Since I wrote *My First Exorcism*, I have witnessed a persistent stream of people—believers and unbelievers alike—asking, sometimes begging, for help in dealing with the demonic influence in their lives. From these experiences, I consistently witness three areas that act as entry points for demons: false religion and impure belief, sexual sins, and drugs. Thus, sexual abuse is often an entry point for demons, as is the abuse of illegal or legal drugs. All are a devilish bending of God's will for selfish purposes. By nature, we all seek to control our own destiny. Yet some perversions are more obvious, and controllable, than others.

This concurs with the Bible. The Bible connects abuses of sex, drugs, and the occult. The Epistle to the Galatians spells out a list of "works of the flesh" (5:19): "sexual immorality, impurity, sensuality, idolatry, sorcery, enmity, strife, jealousy, fits of anger, rivalries, dissensions, divisions, envy, drunkenness, orgies, and things like these" (vv. 19–21). The Greek word *pharmakia* (from which we receive *pharmacy*) is translated as "magic" or "sorcery" in some English versions but also as "drug use" or "incantations" in others. The Revelation of St. John denounces the same practices (Rev. 9:21; 21:8; 22:15). *Pharmakia* seems to have involved "root poisons" that were used at the time to cause abortions, normally administered along with pagan blessings.

In any case, these three categories of sins are often clustered together, indicating their intricate relationship. The grouping is not random. All false religion and impure doctrines stem from the kingdom of darkness. Once again, what are unveiled as entry points for demons are:

> Sexual sins of all sorts, for "every other sin a person commits is outside the body, but the sexually immoral person sins against his own body" (1 Cor. 6:18). Sexual abuse involves sins done against us. That's one tragic way that the devil enters the lives of innocent victims. Yet the more common form of entry is sexual sins to which we expose ourselves including fornication, adultery, homosexuality, bestiality, incest, pornography, and

the list goes on. Although temptation to such sins hovers around us like a flock of vultures, the Lord empowers us to prevent it from nesting in our souls, as we flee to Him as our refuge and He grants us ways of escape (1 Cor. 10:13).

False teaching of all kinds (1 Tim. 4:11–16), for the devil is characterized as a murderous liar. False teaching robs us of our only source of help in the spiritual battle. It's even referred to as the "deep things of Satan" (Rev. 2:24). False doctrine convinces victims that God is evil and the devil is good, or that God's holy Word is erroneous and unreliable (vv. 18–29). It leads the gullible and desperate into paths of unrighteousness as they tap into twisted reason, ungodly ideas, and anti-Christian religion. Our minds are putty in the hands of the devil as soon as we allow the Holy Bible to cease being the pillar grounding all our thoughts and decisions. So, too, wrong information about God and His answers to the devil's schemes is the chief way the devil cripples our trust in the Lord's means of salvation. False teaching can even lead sincere practitioners of the ministry of deliverance astray. For example, those who desire a magic solution to demonic oppression or a Christian phrase as a kind of spell for guaranteeing a successful exorcism get such silly ideas from "Christian" sources. Instead, God's will is always done when we rely upon His Word and prayerfully and humbly approach the task before us.

Drug use, including alcohol abuse (Eph. 5:18). Drugs cloud our ability to think and diminish our effectiveness in the battle. We can't wage war when we're intoxicated or fuzzy-minded. The abuse and overuse of illegal or legal drugs is often symptomatic of other spiritual concerns such as lack of trust in Christ and His Word. It doesn't help that the surrounding culture, which doesn't appreciate value in suffering, tempts and enables those who struggle mentally, physically, and emotionally to uncritically incorporate drugs into their daily lives in hopes of finding support. Non-Christian medical doctors are quick to prescribe these helps while faithful pastors are often shy to offer any advice to the contrary, lest they speak outside of their field of expertise. But the fact is that spirituality is not an isolated, self-contained compartment of the human experience. Spirituality is the foundational underpinning and matrix joining together body, mind, and soul. The use of drugs can compromise one's ability to control oneself or permit the Holy Spirit to maintain control. Sometimes it completely surrenders vital territory to the evil one, who then greedily takes over. Marijuana, for example, entices us to use it to "check out" of our problems instead of engaging them and using the Lord as our strength. Dismissing the spiritual benefits of suffering under the guise of showing compassion explains the medical decisions at various stages of life.

It's a sad reality that nowadays, when the elderly are admitted into palliative care, the trend is to automatically give them morphine. Help them die by minimizing the pain. Nobody seriously asks them to share their thoughts. When was the last time a loved one second-guessed the expert's opinion? Although not identical with assisted suicide, the decision is driven by the same line of reasoning. But pain and suffering aren't something to be avoided at all costs. Robbing the dying of their reasoning abilities so that they can experience a more comfortable end may be a treacherous trade-off. Let's not kid ourselves. We don't know what's happening in those minds and souls. Those who appear unresponsive can often hear more than we think. And the elderly are some of the best Christian warriors. Why on earth would we deprive these spiritual athletes of the ability to tackle that last stretch? In the broader unseen spiritual war, their fighting efforts are vitally important. No one has the right to deprive these mighty yet vulnerable warriors the opportunity to fight with lucid prayer. And yet, their loved ones are often told by a medical professional that "there's nothing left to do" and "they're no longer there."

But Jesus says, "If anyone would come after me, let him deny himself and take up his cross and follow me" (Matt. 16:24). Pain helps us fight. Suffering causes us to pray. The heavy burdens of life drive us to our knees in humility and repentance, and we rise from this dust heap with renewed faith. Drugs alter our minds. Our minds are connected to our hearts and souls.

Don't take this the wrong way. Drugs can wisely be used as a gift of God. Like alcohol (1 Tim. 5:23), they have a place. But they are not neutral. They do more than just ease the pain.

As mentioned earlier, approximately one-quarter of US adults struggle with mental health issues, and many presumably rely solely upon pharmaceuticals to cope with life. One can expect lots of overuse in prescribed medicines. In North America, the legalization of more drugs and the fact that illegal drugs have never been easier to attain should put the Church on full alert.

Normally, in suspected demoniacs, one finds a history of any one of these three vices present, if not all three combined.

It's no surprise, then, that when the individual is cognizant, a practitioner ought to walk them through a rite of confession and absolution, reminding them of the promise God made to them when He baptized them, especially when the voices in their head tell them that they are worthless and useless. But in the case of possession, you are now dealing with a separate identity—an entity that needs to be exorcised.

7

HOW TO EXORCISE
A DEMON

Once all the prep work has been done, and the spiritual problem can't be reduced to one of weak oppression, we are ready to explore the weeds of demon possession. A whole bunch of new questions arise, including, Can the devil be cast out by using a certain method? At what point do you take action, and how? Friedrich Balduin gives us some pretty helpful and specific guidelines:

> When a true possession is recognized, let the poor be committed to the care of a minister of the Church who teaches sound doctrine, is of a blameless life, who does nothing for the sake of financial gain, but does everything from the soul.
>
> Let him diligently inquire what kind of life the possessed one led up to this point, and lead him through the law to the recognition of his sins. If he was previously pious, let him console him that even God sometimes leaves His people in

the power of the devil for certain causes, which the histories of Job and Paul testify.

After this admonition or consolation has taken place, let also the works of a natural physician be used, who will cleanse him . . . with the appropriate medicines. For it has been ascertained that possessed people frequently suffer from a double disease, namely of body and of soul, for example, insanity, grief, weariness of life, desperation.

It is not necessary to bring him into the temple [church] (but can help depending on circumstances and pastoral care and discretion) in the sight of the people, as the custom is for many. Let the confession of the Christian faith be once required of him; let him be taught concerning the works of the devil destroyed by Christ; let him be sent back faithfully to this Destroyer of Satan, Jesus Christ; let an exhortation be set up to faith in Christ, to prayers, to penitence.

Let ardent prayers be poured forth to God, not only by the ministers of the Church, but also by the whole Church. Let these prayers be conditioned, if the liberation should happen, for God's glory and the salvation of the possessed person, for this is an evil of the body.

With the prayers let fasting be joined (see Matt. 17:21) and alms by friends of the possessed person (Tob. 12:8–9).

In summary, all things happen by prayers and the Word. If the [desired] effect does not immediately follow, remember that not even the adjurations of exorcists are always efficacious. And since this benefit of going out [of the devil] is bodily, therefore, in prayers of this kind, the will of God must always be included. Thus He hears them not according to our will but according to what's best for us. But the fact that our prayers for the possessed are not heard immediately, and as we ask, is due, among other things, to the unbelief of the possessed ones, who do not approach with certain faith, asking liberation from God. Therefore Christ said to the parent of a certain demon-possessed one, "If you can believe the liberation of your son, it will happen" (Mark 9:19–24).[1]

This prefatory introduction sets the stage for the steps that need to be taken and should be carefully followed.

Procedure in the Case of Actual Possession

Step 1: Choose a Confidential Team of Helpers

A practitioner or exorcist needs to avoid any "Lone Ranger" tendencies and should make sure to recruit a team of mature clergy and Christians who are committed to praying and fasting together. God works through a body, and no one member has all the gifts. Besides, "iron sharpens iron, and one man sharpens another" (Prov. 27:17).

The fact that this ministry is a function of the wider Church implies that it should only be conducted with proper authorization. Ideally, bishops or ecclesiastical supervisors have been consulted and offered their blessing, support, and advice on your engagement with a demoniac. Even if these leaders are uncomfortable with the subject, they can, at the very least, offer access to networks of those known to be especially experienced in this field. "It is important that the pastoral carer not exceed his/her authority or expertise, and that he/she take care to avoid manipulating people through ritual or coercing them into going beyond what they are ready for—which could be a form of ritual abuse."[2] Additionally, working with a team shares this heavy responsibility of carefully navigating in this less-trodden area of ministry. It's important that there are witnesses, advisers, and

1. Mayes, "Demon Possession and Exorcism in Lutheran Orthodoxy," 332–33. Used by permission.
2. LCA, *Rites and Resources for Pastoral Care*, 139.

protectors, especially if the demoniac exhibits any violent behavior.

Exclude curious spectators or tourists of all kinds. Any participants that do not have a clear role to play can sabotage the endeavor. Keep all skeptics away. You can't be distracted by feeling obligated to prove that your diagnosis is right or your path ahead is wise. The best preparation of this team is ensuring that all are solid and orthodox in their Christian beliefs and have examined their hearts and lives and confessed their sins to God. Only then are they rightly equipped to pray for protection, wisdom, and guidance by the Holy Spirit in their navigation of this dark terrain.

If humility and unity in the Faith are lacking, the assailant will find wicked ways of causing division and distractions. One priest was taken off guard when the devil publicly exposed his secret love affair through the mouth of the demoniac. Incidentally, he had never repented of these sexual sins, and the shocking exposure paralyzed him from continuing with the spiritual intervention.[3] He was so ashamed and rattled that he could not perform his duties. The others in the room were equally horrified and lost their footing in that spiritual battle. The devil knows our weak spots. We will have skeletons in our closets. It's always a win-win when we let our Lord into those secret places. He removes all the stinking bones that can poison godly faith and hinder Christian ministry.

But when all sins are confessed and forgiven, the devil can't use them against us by smearing our reputation before the heavenly courts since "as far as the east is from the west, so far does he remove our transgressions from us" (Ps. 103:12). Therefore, "If we confess our sins, he is faithful and just to

---

3. Vogl, *Begone, Satan!*, 31.

forgive us our sins and to cleanse us from all unrighteousness" (1 John 1:9).

Even though it's best that the in-person group be kept small (two or three people), the leader can always feel free to recruit others to pray both before and after the event. Certainly, pastors need to take care not to break confidence, but their confessional seal does not preclude prayers for those who wish to remain nameless.

Avoid recordings and streaming, since the footage can be used for devilish and twisted purposes. There remains a thoughtful debate over whether any sacred events should be captured on video. It may be inconceivable to many of us that televised church services are controversial. But the Church has always rightfully wrestled with appropriate use of technology in the deployment of its services. Even electricity was once considered unsuitable in a sanctuary, since artificial light was seen as implicitly problematic to the ministry of the one true Light, Christ our Lord, in that space. Jesus is real and not fake. Let's not tempt people to think otherwise, even subconsciously. Is there any spiritual difference between hearing the Word through speakers via microphones versus directly from the mouth of the preacher? Even if you disagree with the logic or suggested concerns, the idea that sacred acts are being conveyed through potentially unbecoming mediums that don't do justice to the mystery of the occasion is a valid one.[4]

An exorcism can't be exactly described as *sacred*, but it weirdly belongs to this realm of the sacred. Accordingly, none of those involved—even the antagonists—are to be

4. The argument that there is no such thing as a neutral medium, and that some media are therefore more appropriate for the conveyance of the sacred in terms of holy ideas and spiritual activity, is well articulated in Neil Postman, *Amusing Ourselves to Death* (Penguin, 1985).

exploited. A unique kind of chivalry should be shown by exorcists, who aren't to celebrate or glorify the event in unseemly ways. Do not succumb to the pathetic and desperate temptation to publicize an exorcism for the sake of evangelism, or even to kill any doubts in the mind of the possessed one later, since they would have been oblivious to what had just transpired. We may think, *If only others could see what I am seeing, they would believe!* But even Jesus did not create faith in hearts by miracles. In fact, some chased Him out of the village after an exorcism (Matt. 8:34). "Do not give dogs what is holy, and do not throw your pearls before pigs, lest they trample them underfoot and turn to attack you" (7:6).

Step 2: Choose an Appropriate Time and Location

An exorcism isn't necessarily an emergency and can often be planned beforehand. Now, don't get me wrong. Some demons seek to destroy the body. But even in the New Testament account of the son who was possessed from childhood and was often cast "into fire and into water" (Mark 9:22), he survived the devil's murderous attempts for years. The length of every life remains in the sovereign hands of God (Job 14:5). This is a great comfort when spiritual caregivers wonder whether the safety or destiny of a demoniac is dependent upon their decisions and prayers.

This is not meant as permission to deprioritize somebody suffering with demonism. Some cases require immediate action, such as those in which the demonically oppressed have suicidal tendencies. But for the most part, in my experience, the demon has made the host its home and is not eager to leave. The thing has been there a long time, and so deliverance isn't necessarily time sensitive. That being said, don't wait too long, especially for those who sincerely desire freedom from demonic bondage and are willing to pick up their cross and follow Jesus. For Roman Catholics, the bureaucracy often gets in the way. It takes a long time to pass requests up their chain of command. But evangelical Christians often have the opposite problem: overly eager and responsive clergy behaving as if, without their immediate heroic aid, special presence, and unique talents, all will be lost. Moreover, some insist upon uncovering demons where there aren't any. Disheartened with the discovery that no exorcism is actually necessary, they fake it, fighting with phantoms and causing a lot of damage.[5]

As a chaplain, I worked with a medical doctor who converted to Christianity after personally observing demonic displays in a mutual "client." I refused to exorcise the oppressed man because he didn't desire deliverance as much as he should have. With great anxiety, the doctor was stupefied that I had not "fixed his demon problem" before his patient drove home from work. He was also mystified by how calm and relaxed I was in discussing it. He thought that the guy would end up in a car wreck. I assured the physician that his patient had been living with this demon for years. I said, "Don't panic. It's not like the movies. He's not at risk. He's not an out-of-control zombie." The devil doesn't want to attract too much attention to himself, after all.[6]

---

5. When regular temptations to sin are attributed to demons in some Christian circles (e.g., demon of smoking, demon of drinking, demon of generational curses), one consequence is that sinners blame the devil for their behavior as opposed to taking responsibility for it themselves.

6. Certainly, there is an increasing number of accounts of demonism in public due to better access to information and a friendliness toward the occult and the devil, but again, generally, the devil opts for subtle methods of penetrating lives with his presence. For example, *The Satanic Bible* by Anton Szandor LaVey doesn't consist of instructions on sorcery or human sacrifices but reiterates seemingly innocuous humanistic wisdom. The message can be summarized as caring for oneself above all else (i.e., egoism), in contrast to Jesus's expectation that we live our lives in servitude of others, mimicking Him.

I refuse to simply race into the life of an alleged demoniac, conducting a crisis intervention like a kind of spiritual ER doctor. Some are so desperate that they have offered to pay me and cover all my travel expenses if I would just visit them. Instead, these people need a local pastor—a spiritual *family* doctor. Otherwise, long-term care after exorcism won't happen. Besides, it's incumbent upon the entire community of Christian supporters—the Church—to get involved by praying, fasting, monitoring, and encouraging. Church ministry is always team ministry.

In short, any help I offer is always conditional on connecting a person with a local Bible-based and Christ-centered Christian congregation. Sadly, when hearing this, many shrink away frustrated. They want deliverance *from* their fears and internal prisons without being delivered *to* the One who eternally satisfies and frees. Jesus can work however He pleases, but He prefers to work through His Church. Jesus promised St. Peter that the gates of hell would not prevail against this organic body and organization (Matt. 16:18). Those who choose to cut themselves off from this family don't have the same hope.

In terms of the location of the exorcism, a church sanctuary is ideal for practical and symbolic reasons. It reinforces the idea that the ministry of deliverance is a corollary of wider Christian ministry. I have found it much easier to conduct acts of deliverance in sacred places. The demon is so uncomfortable there that it may flee without much effort. Make sure that appropriate safety precautions are observed. A deliverance often concludes with physical collapse as the demon leaves, like a child tossing their dress-up clothes onto the floor once they are done playing. I recommend that the individual kneel, such as at the edge of a chancel, surrounded by prayerful supporters nearby. That way, he or she can be easily caught. I always wear my stole as a reminder of the office of Christ, and whenever I lay my hand upon the individual, I try to use my stole. The Eastern Orthodox sew an extra long piece of cloth onto their priestly stoles to make this easier. This act exhibits that the shepherding hand of Jesus is the one touching His precious lamb.

Insisting that the severely oppressed or possessed person make the appointment at the church ensures their seriousness. The devil will resist entry into a church with all his might. At the same time, he's willing to put up with it sometimes, as part of the deceptive games that he plays. But it's always a bad sign whenever anyone stays away from church. In any case, the individual needs to be committed. When they do what you ask, it shows they are. Demons habitually warn the individual in a dream or vision not to come. As I mentioned before, a number of times I've learned that the person had been told to stay away from me. This is normal. Don't be disappointed if they don't show up to the meeting. It may just not be the right time yet. Trust in God.

Step 3: Carefully Monitor the Situation

Everyone on the caregiving team is the eyes and ears of Christ's body as they continuously monitor the attitudes and behavior, postures and gestures, and actions and reactions of the oppressed or possessed person. With that in mind, together you operate according to four basic principles.[7]

1. *React to what is manifested.* Have no predetermined personal agenda nor carry any presumptions on how you think things will unfold. Instead, utilize the Word of God and prayer at every twist and turn of

---

7. Developed by my friend and colleague Dr. John Kleinig.

the forecasted demonic encounter. Even at the stage of asking certain questions, you may find evidence of the demonic worm awakening. When you are ready to pull it out, you can insist that the individual recite the Lord's Prayer or read Scripture specific to Jesus as victor over the devil. They won't be able to, and the demon will likely manifest itself. But be careful; if you are not comfortable or prepared, and you push too hard, you may be taken off guard. The worm exits the hole, and it may take a while for it to find its way back into hiding. You may end up having a face-off with a demon and panic or become speechless.

2. *Pray as you listen to the oppressed attempt to answer your questions, confess their sins, or follow your instructions.* Then, if the person comes under the influence of a hostile power during this personal ministry and starts to speak in profane ways, rebuke the evil spirit as Christ did in response to Peter in Mark 8:33. Speak the following words of rebuke from the rite of baptism: "Depart from [Name], you unclean spirit, and make way for the Holy Spirit, in the name of the Father and of the Son and of the Holy Spirit. Amen." Or else say, "In the name of the Lord Jesus, I command you to leave [Name]."[8]

3. *Rely on the guidance of the Holy Spirit and God's Word the whole time.* It's not a science but an art. Remember, each demon is unique. Different liturgical tools and Scriptures resonate with different demons. When using a rite, the portions that aggravate the demonic entity ought to be repeated. I have even used the ancient Litany as a way of monitoring responses of a suspected

8. LCA, *Rights and Resources for Pastoral Care*, 143.

demoniac. Certain petitions have a stronger effect on some demons than others. The phrase "trampling Satan under our feet" is particularly potent. The ceaseless repetition of sacred phraseology, such as holy names for Jesus (i.e., Son of God and King of Kings), confessions of faith in Him like "Jesus is Lord," and versions of the Jesus Prayer—"Lord, have mercy on me, a sinner"— have proven very effective for me.

4. *End with a blessing in the name of the Triune God.* Rejoice in what God has achieved. Try not to be flabbergasted or spooked at any point during this battle. Simply celebrate the victory of Jesus.

In terms of the governing philosophy underlying this ministry, much of the interaction and battle involves recalling and proclaiming scriptural truths to all in attendance. This includes reminding everyone of their baptism and their Christian identity established there, for "your names are written in heaven" (Luke 10:20).

Regarding non-Christians or those not yet baptized, this means announcing Christ's glorious death as the source of the devil's defeat and their source of hope. The devil is a thief and a liar. He needs to be rebuked with the truth. He is a squatter in another's home. He must be told that he is no longer welcome. Evil entities need to be reminded that Jesus is *their* Lord as King of the universe and that they remain subjected to Him in every way, shape, and form. Jesus says, "I died, and behold I am alive forevermore, and I have the keys of Death and Hades" (Rev. 1:18). They shudder at this message (James 2:19).

When you get tired of reciting Scripture and praying, hymn and psalm singing are a good default position. The Word of Christ will torment demons so much that they will eventually depart due to the agonizing pain they experience, although the timing of their exodus is in accordance with the sovereign divine will of God. However, beware: The serpents may appear to have fled but actually have slithered back into hiding. Even though the possessed may have altered their previous disposition by falling unconscious or asleep, vomiting, or feeling dehydrated, these are not certain signs that the job is complete. Yet the delivered demoniac will know when the mission has been accomplished, if they are honest. They can feel the difference inside.[9] Any hesitation or inability to join you in prayer or articulate divine Scripture is a guarantee that the demons have not yet fled.

Outline of a Rite for Deliverance

There are many rites available in the library of Christendom, but all good ones basically follow this format, which may or may not lead to an exorcism but always to some degree of deliverance.[10] Each session is best ended with some parts of the rite that I have outlined below, particularly a Scripture reading, the Lord's Prayer, intercessory prayer by those present, and, when the pastor is present, a blessing with the laying on of hands. The procedures suggested under the main headings of the rite are recommendations and will vary according to the peculiarities of the situation. Prayerful discernment should always govern the choices made.

---

9. Although feelings are a bad way of doing theology, sometimes when it comes to this ministry, they can be a real gift. As is the case of chills, goose bumps, not feeling right, bad feelings, and so on.

10. The rite I describe below is loosely based on the LCA Rite for Spiritual Oppression; see *Rites and Resources for Pastoral Care*, 138–45.

Invocation in the Name of the One True God

In the name of the Father and of the Son (make the sign of the cross) and of the Holy Spirit.[11] Amen.

Opening Prayers

These may be prayers for Trinitarian protection, acknowledging the Father (who is sovereign Creator), the Son (who suffered on the cross and conquered darkness), and the Holy Spirit (who brings new life and strength for sanctified living).

Psalm 91 may be used as a prayer of protection for the person from the powers of darkness.

Scriptures and Instruction

The witness of Scripture proclaiming the victory of Christ over Satan needs to be clearly read and preached. In the case of oppressed or possessed Christians, the significance of baptism as the sacramental event of death and burial with Christ should be the practical focus. This offers the chance to speak out loud the reality that the oppressed or possessed is inhabited by an impostor. An exorcism takes back what is rightfully the Lord's.

Confession, Renunciation, and Absolution

The person is encouraged to confess any sins on their conscience and helped to articulate those sins. This may lead to acknowledging and renouncing the devil's activity and the person's sins associated with the occult. The pastor then forgives them all their sins in the stead and by the command of the Lord Jesus Christ.

---

11. Making the sign of the cross when speaking the name of the Son is an important and powerful outward gesture that is potent for both the possessed and the demon to see. Having a visible crucifix in hand is also a good idea.

Word of God

Read the "Big Five" demon texts while sharing brief comments. Other texts describing Jesus's authority over the devil may be better selections, depending on the context.

Mark 1:21–28

Mark 5:1–20

Mark 7:24–30

Mark 9:14–29

Luke 13:10–17

Christian Creed

The person confesses the Christian Faith and allegiance to the Triune God using the words of the Apostles' Creed, as in the rite of baptism.

The Our Father

The person is asked to join in praying the Lord's Prayer. Special emphasis may be given to the last two petitions. After all, one of the earliest translations states "deliver us from the evil one" as opposed to "deliver us from evil."

Deliverance

If the demon has not yet revealed its ugly face, the pastor may lay his hands on the person (and even anoint them with oil). The pastor makes the following or a similar proclamation: "As a servant of Christ and by His authority, I set you free from the devil, in the name of the Father and of the Son (at this moment, trace the sign of the cross on the forehead or in the air in front of the demoniac) and of the Holy Spirit. Amen." Conversely, a prayer for deliverance based on John 16:23–24 can be used.

Prayers

Prayers to or for the Holy Spirit are spoken, asking that God would fill the person's heart and control their life. The pastor may lay hands (even using the tip of their stole, if wearing one) on the individual's head. This may go on for a long time. After the demons have left, proceed with the next step.

Token

The person may be presented with a token of their allegiance to the Triune God, such as a crucifix, a portion of Scripture, or a copy of a prayer or hymn. The token may be blessed for the person's use, and the presentation accompanied by the speaking of a Scripture verse and/or instruction on its use.

Instruction on expectations regarding the Christian life and worship in the Church ought to follow, since the delivered is obviously wondering, *What happens next?*

Conclusion

Prayers of thanksgiving are said, yet with one eye open to monitor the individual for any further strange behavior, since sometimes the work is not yet complete, as in the case of multiple demons. A hymn or song celebrating Christ as victor and the ultimate spiritual warrior is an appropriate way of praising God to the hosts of heaven and hordes of hell. A final word of blessing, perhaps incorporating words from Mark 16:17–18, along with the laying on of hands should occur before everybody goes home.[12]

---

12. LCA, *Rites and Resources for Pastoral Care*, 138–45.

So there you have it: a simple way of delivering demons in rare and extreme cases. Yet even when dealing with moderate or mild oppression, these steps and practices can help you determine the level of severity. At the very least, they offer a chance to worship, one that wouldn't have happened otherwise. Worst-case scenario: you're embarrassed that things didn't roll the way you'd expected. Yet even there, for those unpresumptuous and humble in heart, what's the big deal? I'd rather be scorned on judgment day for making a misdiagnosis and choosing to risk my reputation for a hurting brother or sister than be scolded for taking the easy way out. God wants us to pray "at all times in the Spirit, with all prayer and supplication. To that end, keep alert with all perseverance, making supplication for all the saints" (Eph. 6:18). Even though it's the devil that gives us that chance, I'll take it every time!

8

AFTERCARE

Just like a first responder at the scene of a car accident, a practitioner of exorcism responds in certain prescribed ways. For example, you take control of the emergency and deal with the vital issues at hand. After the patients are stabilized, they need to recover in the hospital and will require lots of care.

When it comes to the ministry of deliverance, the aftercare is as important as the initial intervention. If the exorcism has not taken place at the residence of the demoniac, the home should be visited as soon as possible. If the person believes that their house is haunted, the rite for blessing a house should be conducted with special emphasis on the reading of Psalm 91 and the placement of a cross or crucifix in the house while reciting the Apostles' Creed.

All occult items, religious amulets, or questionable objects that have any suspicious or sentimental attachment to the individual should be renounced and destroyed by fire, not just tossed in the trash. This act is practical, so that it's no longer recoverable, but also symbolic; it's sent back to hell, where it belongs. "And a number of those who had practiced magic arts brought their books together and burned them in the sight of all. And they counted the value of them and found it came to fifty thousand pieces of silver" (Acts 19:19).

Ideally, the delivered individual oversees this symbolic gesture, exemplifying that they comprehend that they—not someone else—are responsible for their issue. Healthy signs of taking their spiritual condition seriously include renouncing evil practices or items. Many throw out heavy metal albums that depict satanic images and contain sinful lyrics. By observing these choices, the exorcist can determine the degree to which the individual is dedicated to staying "clean" and committed to getting help.

The individual should be eager to receive Christian prayers at the site of deliverance or conducted at their home, including the singing of hymns and psalms. But all the while, the exorcist is continually monitoring the behavior of the delivered one, ensuring that religious imagery is present in the home, along with Bibles, hymnals, and sacred music; at the very least, insisting that copies of the Lord's Prayer and Apostles' Creed are available. I once ministered to a soldier who carried a folded liturgical Compline service in his back pocket, and he would read and recite it whenever he felt devilish attacks while carrying out his military duties.

After careful follow-up and surveillance for the next few days, the caregivers can slowly retreat so as to circumvent unhealthy dependence or an alluring temptation to become someone's personal savior. Ongoing care is the responsibility of the larger Christian community, and, when appropriate, Christian mental health professionals and a medical doctor should join the mix.

Avoiding Pitfalls

In terms of the practitioner's head and heart space, the following deserve special attention.

Firstly, because the devil is a deceiver who seduces through his disguise as an angel of light, anyone engaging in this kind of ministry ought to take great care to avoid the following:

> Credulous obsession with demons *or* skepticism regarding them.
>
> Labeling all inexplicable phenomena as demonic *or* accepting everything "spiritual" as a gift from the Holy Spirit.
>
> Fear of involvement in the ministry of deliverance *or* the presumption of expertise in it.[1]

One cannot overstate how important it is for the caregiver to seek the counsel and support of other Christians, especially clergy, before engaging in the ministry of deliverance.

Lucifer—which means "bearer of light"—is skilled at blinding with his false light by enticing us to shine the spotlight upon ourselves and highlight our own abilities. Contrast this with the Holy Spirit, who conducts Himself as the quiet one of the Holy Trinity, directing the attention away from Himself and pointing us instead to Jesus, who is the Way to the Father. He creates faith in the sacrificial work of the Savior. We need to do the same.

The ministry of deliverance is to be approached with a humble and reverent attitude that subjects the human will and any egoism to the throne of God. Be on guard against self-proclaimed exorcists or those flaunting "special" spiritual

---

1. LCA, *Rites and Resources for Pastoral Care*, 139.

gifts. Just like the fruits of a tree are meant to be eaten by others, and the tree from which they sprout is largely ignorant of their existence, spiritual gifts and talents are best identified by other people. The Vatican has an advantage here with their pool of vetted, trained, and experienced specialists, whereas in Protestantism, there is way too much independent action and eager enthusiasm to seek out demons by those with little accountability for their man-made ministries.

Secondly, a practitioner or exorcist must have tireless patience and unwavering faith. Sometimes an exorcism takes a lot of time, and it's a waiting game. Like a Christian caregiver sitting at the bedside of a dying church member, you may feel like you can't offer any more prayers or words, but your presence is still indispensable. It's the same with an exorcism.

Praying the Lord's Prayer quietly or out loud should never be undervalued. It acknowledges and taps into the network of angels and hosts of heaven who join the practitioner, along with our High Priest, Jesus the Christ, the Chief Exorcist.

Thirdly, even though there's no cookie-cutter solution to treating the oppressed and possessed, avoid becoming overly creative. A nonlegalistic approach to liturgical rites and resources doesn't mean that the ministry of deliverance is left open to the imagination (1 Cor. 6:12). Practitioners may be free to use different approaches but must ensure that each is Christ-centered and faith-driven. Everything not from faith is sin (Rom. 14:23). All rites and ceremonies need to be dependent upon God's Word rather than based in a right ritual performance. The Lord doesn't work through magic. He works through faith and prayer.

The rule of thumb is to use the old tools that have been handed to us through the Church, instead of anything new.

This sacred equipment has stood the test of time. It's also not presumptuous. Thus, employ a systematic approach using Scripture passages and ancient prayers. There is some debate over the use of "sacramentals" as efficacious, such as holy water and salt, which convey obvious symbolic importance. If these are used, they must be treated clearly as supports to the Word and not as a kind of superstitious solution. I know of one priest who urged a man to drink consecrated water whenever he felt the devil around! Even when such prescriptions seem to be effectual, the problem with "doing whatever works" is that it may be a malicious snare. Although the devil can't cast out the devil (Matt. 12:25–27), he can make it appear as if he's been defeated while, in reality, he remains the puppeteer active behind the scenes.

Fourthly, practitioners need to appreciate the fact that they're to act in a professional manner while operating with constraints on their knowledge. No one will ever come close to understanding how this realm works. It's not for humans to know. It's not for humans to explore. Some exorcists have made the mistake of trying to gather information from a demon by demanding answers from it. For example, some ask questions to discover the entry point or insist on knowing the demon's name to gain more control over it. But when it comes to truth and lies, "wherever the corpse is, there the vultures will gather" (Matt. 24:28). Demons can pretend to have subjected themselves to your will and lie in response to questions that you demand they answer. In my opinion, commanding a demon to answer your question, even in the name of Jesus, is unnecessary, dangerous, and an abuse of authority.

Jesus doesn't attach His promises to any of these kinds of tactical strategies. He promises deliverance from the devil, according to His divine will. My approach is to stick to the script of a biblical and Christ-based rite—the use of sacred phraseology and prayer. Similarly, shy away from long, drawn-out, or theatrical rituals. The goal is to deliver the possessed, not interrogate the demon or make a show for spectators.

Practitioners are just humble soldiers carrying out a specific task and assigned mission. It's never personal. They're just doing their job: shoot to kill. They don't need to know all the enemy's details: personal history, family life, and so on. When it comes to the demoniac, the less that's known about the beast, and the less dialogue exchanged, the better. Besides, treating a demon like an alien specimen to be examined is not only potentially treacherous but also immature. Consider how visitors to a zoo approach a caged, vicious beast. They interact with it while maintaining a healthy reluctance to get too close. Only a fool would mock, tease, or throw stones at it. It's stronger than a person, despite being restrained behind bars. As mentioned earlier, there's a way in which we show a kind of respect for the dark sphere, not by any means in a sense of revering or honoring it but rather acknowledging that the battle taking place is a mysterious one in which we ought to feel out of place and even, rightly understood, unworthy, as the spheres of holiness and unholiness collide.

Being professional also includes being focused. Soldiers are trained to be calm and in control of their emotions when at war. They avoid unnecessary movements and actions when on patrol and on guard. They also know that it's silly to try to be the hero by relying on their own abilities. They put their faith in their equipment. Likewise, in the ministry of deliverance you can't rely on your own personal worthiness, ego, virtues, experience, or even giftedness. You must trust only in Christ. For example, I have already shared how you should avoid deliberate eye contact with a demon who can seduce and frighten you with its Medusa effect. You'll never win that staring contest. Instead, focus on Jesus and fix your eyes upon Him (Heb. 12:2) as the one and only Exorcist. He is the source of all true power. He enables you to minister. Outside of Him, you are nothing.

There's great comfort and relief in the fact that power resides only in Jesus, whose "grace is sufficient for [us], for [His] power is made perfect in [our] weakness" (2 Cor. 12:9). Just like sage pastors take comfort in the fact that the growth or decline of their churches is not a matter of their own failures or successes, when they are practicing faithfully and never diluting doctrine, the results are always the fruits of a spiritual wrestling match that remains in the hands of almighty God. So, too, exorcists can rest assured that they are just humble vessels of the Lord. Jesus and His angels are the ones who do the real work.

Ongoing Care for the Delivered

The necessary aftercare offered to the demonically delivered is articulated well by the Lutheran Church:

> The Ministry of deliverance from spiritual oppression oc-
> curs in and through the regular divine service of the church,
> particularly in the confession and absolution, in the sacra-
> ment of baptism, and in the sacrament of Holy Communion.
> Where people remain burdened, personal pastoral ministry
> needs to be extended. This personal ministry needs to be
> closely connected with the sacrament of baptism, and either
> prepares people for baptism or deals with ongoing spiritual
> oppression of people after baptism. This personal ministry
> is always subordinate to the divine service of the church.[2]

2. LCA, *Rites and Resources for Pastoral Care*, 138.

Remember that the devil hates the presence of Christ. And Jesus enters us through the Word and sacraments of the Lord's Church. The blood of the Lamb sets us free from the power of the evil one (Rev. 12:11). Jesus says, "Drink of it, all of you, for this is my blood of the covenant, which is poured out for many for the forgiveness of sins" (Matt. 26:27–28).

Inasmuch as the Church is the body of Christ and temple of the Holy Spirit, each Christian functions as a kind of microcosm of Jesus and that same temple. So the best way of keeping Satan away is to heap the coals of God's Word upon his horrid head by grounding delivered, oppressed, or recovering demoniacs in the life of the Church. It's absolutely essential that they become altogether active in church in a way more intense than the average Christian: deep Bible study, catechesis, heightened home devotional practices, weekly and biweekly worship services, a developed and scheduled prayer life, and, when appropriate, immediate preparation for holy baptism and the Holy Eucharist.

Christian brothers and sisters should be assigned to these individuals to help coach, track, and keep them accountable to this rigid spiritual program. Full participation in healthy Christian community among other Christians, who befriend the recovering, is a way of normalizing the abnormal in order to reduce any unfortunate but natural prejudice from others. We all have our sins, burdens, and trials, and while some are more visible and peculiar than others, none make us less righteous and acceptable in the sight of God. We are equally covered by the blood of Christ. "Therefore, since we have been justified by faith, we have peace with God through our Lord Jesus Christ" (Rom. 5:1).

The ministry of deliverance involves both proactive and reactive strategies. If you have ants inside your house, you need to do two things to cope: exterminate those that are there with insecticide and take measures to prevent them from returning, like maintaining a clean kitchen floor. It's the same with the homes of our hearts. After "haunted houses" receive a house blessing, I encourage the placement of Christian imagery on walls, the playing of Christian hymnody and music, and frequent family devotions in which the Holy Scriptures are read aloud. I even advised one man to listen to the audible Bible through his headphones while sleeping. This helped him immensely in controlling the onslaught of demonic voices in his head.

Trusting that God loves others more than you ever could will definitely help avert any temptation toward acting as the savior of the struggling individual—and the accompanying compassion fatigue when they lean on you with more weight than you can handle. Many of those recovering from demonism have a whole slew of other relational, emotional, and mental problems. These will unintentionally find ways of pulling caregivers into the deep and dangerous pits of their broken lives. Yet the only One with whom they can really share their pains is Jesus Christ, through whose wounds they have lasting healing (Isa. 53:4–5).

We may want to protect them out of pride for a deliverance for which we take credit. Sometimes we lack faith in our Lord, forgetting that He can do a much better job managing their problems than we can. These children of God need to be led to their heavenly Father, for they have already been equipped with the tools to cope through His Son—or at least will be once they are baptized or return to the promises God has made to them in their baptism. They are already strong and victorious over the evil one. Yet they're like a baby holding a bazooka. They are newborn soldiers who don't realize the immense power at the tip of their fingers. They need some training. They need Christian instruction. Neglecting to recognize—through wavering faith—the power that is ours makes us lamentably vulnerable to the wily ways of the enemy.

With Christian maturity comes the ability to endure the inevitable counterattacks of the devil via his two persuasive weapons, which instill fear and incite a sense of hopelessness: accusation and condemnation. The most spiritually advanced Christians know that the only solid solution to these imputations is the forgiveness of sins and the strength we find in Christ alone. He was tempted in every way that we are but did not sin (Heb. 4:15–16), overcoming the devil at every twist and turn of His battle (Matt. 4:1–11).

So by whispering discouraging thoughts into our minds, the evil foe does all he can to deflect us from Christ's God-pleasing death, which has made satisfaction for all our sin. All stakeholders in a deliverance, then, need to be on their toes and ready for a repeat of the mission, especially within a few days afterward, as this snake, with his insatiable hunger to consume that which isn't his, conspires to regain lost territory. Like a vulnerable person exiting an abusive relationship, there will be mixed feelings of relief and regret, love and hate. And like the baffling but nevertheless real sadness we experience when the Lord destroys our idols, a delivered demoniac may even undergo a period of grief over their loss. A network of Christian friends can help in the mourning process and intercept any bad decision-making.

In general, recovery strategies for the demonically delivered are similar to those recommended to survivors of post-traumatic stress disorder (PTSD); victims are haunted by figurative demons, and even real ones sometimes. Exposing and not denying the problem is the first step to healing and coping.[3] Self-pity empowers evil to take back control. Instead, boldly confronting the issue by admitting that having to live with these ghosts until death as a real possibility is the best way ahead. Patients living with a terminal illness employ a similar approach in coping with their medical condition. It allows them to adopt a positive outlook on life despite the obvious negative pushback. Survivors are to praise God for any blessings in life as a way of putting their problems in an edifying perspective. Distracting ourselves from earthly mammon is a way of overcoming worries and fears of the future.

Practical things that those delivered can do include getting involved in the life of the Church and volunteering in helpful community services. The horizon of their small world is then expanded as they begin to see that there is more to the world than their problems and their demons. Moreover, they realize that they have much to offer others when they seek ways to serve them, something impossible to do when navel-gazing and self-obsession consume their time and energy.

In short, steering away from self and toward others enables these traumatized survivors to see how God has made them to be valuable in the lives of fellow beloved human beings. When a delivered individual is a member of a family, gratitude for the day that God has made includes actively creating and cultivating a positive and thankful Christ-centered home environment. "Finally, brothers, whatever is true, whatever is honorable, whatever is just, whatever is pure, whatever is lovely, whatever is commendable, if there is any excellence, if there is anything worthy of praise, think about these things" (Phil. 4:8). This is all obviously a turnoff

3. As in the film *A Beautiful Mind*, once the protagonist realizes the ghosts in his head are there to stay, he is able to find strategies to live with them—no longer in fear and agony but resiliently.

for the evil one. He'll likely find a more plush and pleasant residence somewhere else in the neighborhood. He'll go for an easier target.

Self-Care for the Caregiver

Immediately after an exorcism, the exorcist will experience an emotional adrenaline rush and feel amazing happiness, marveling at what the Lord has achieved through one's meager mouth and hands (Luke 10:17). But once the devil has recovered from his defeat, he's soon to come after us out of spite and revenge, sometimes targeting our loved ones, friends, and family. This is all normal collateral damage of spiritual war. Don't run and hide from it. Rather, rejoice in these sufferings (Rom. 5:3).

Usually, when we reflect upon the large catch of fish by the disciples when they first recognized Jesus at the Lake of Gennesaret, we assume everything about that day was terrific. After all, these first disciples had witnessed a miracle! They got what they wanted, and even more. Yet it's the unexpected "even more" part that often uproots our lives and upsets our plans. God gave them more than they had hoped for and probably even desired. Their nets began to tear and their boats began to sink (Luke 5:6–7). Imagine the cleanup afterward. Think about the repairs. Consider the logistic nightmare of dealing with that massive haul of fresh fish! Tons of extra work. More sweat and labor means more pain and suffering. Certainly it was all good . . . very good. But it wasn't comfortable, fun, or clean.

Don't be surprised when a Christian victory results in some sorrow shortly afterward. There is a cross tucked away in every blessing. The sooner we realize this, the faster we can rejoice in it.

As a military chaplain deployed overseas, I experienced the temporary loss of my hearing whenever bombs would explode nearby, and I suffered a few scrapes and bruises during ground attacks. Even though I wasn't armed or actively involved in combat, I was impacted nonetheless. Just living in that violent environment meant I was often stressed, thirsty, sleep-deprived, and trekking along in bloodstained boots and a dirty uniform. I even faced some longer-term vexations, such as disturbed sleep patterns and other spiritual, emotional, and psychological repercussions. Almost all soldiers wrestle with these issues after returning from the theater of war—though their injuries vary in degree for each one. In spiritual warfare, too, even those who aren't fighting on the front line can expect some nasty consequences. Likewise, both short- and long-term self-care need to be actively pursued by all those impacted by the exorcism.

Even when my interventions involve only offering advice over the internet or phone, and when I don't reside in physical proximity to the demonic entities, I experience unusual happenings, amplified temptations, and misplaced feelings that can only be attributed to heightened devilish attacks. These are normal signs that you're in the midst of a wider battle. Don't worry; you'll eventually recover from them.

After being entangled in a complicated out-of-town exorcism, I arrived home exhausted. Yet immediately strange things started occurring in my life. For instance, a teenage friend of the family called me up out of the blue, asking to speak together. I knew she had some mental challenges, but this didn't explain the unanticipated query. She said that she'd had a dream in which she'd remembered that I had behaved inappropriately with her at a very specific event we had both attended several years earlier. I was absolutely shocked by this unfounded "memory"—and the curious timing. I had not recollected the event, and she came to realize how her accusation was unquestionably unlikely, given her own description of it. The alleged incident happened at a large, crowded venue, making the assertion impossible.

She was consoled when I denied the allegation. By talking with me, she seemed to start remembering the event more clearly afterward. Because she was a teenager, I was obviously concerned about the fallout of these disturbing suggestions. I spoke with my wife and a social worker friend about how to proceed. I also called the girl's mother, who knew me well. She quickly dismissed the scenario as both illogical and unthinkable. Although the issue didn't evolve any further, the incident took an emotionally and spiritually taxing toll on me for several days.

A number of other such odd attacks occurred within two weeks of my return. At one point, demonic temptations and accusatory voices inside of me were so strong that, while driving to work, I pulled over to the side of the road and rebuked the devil out loud. That fixed it. God took care of me, but still, it was all rather tiring.

Sometimes we encounter troubles with our spouse, or our children get attacked. Physical illness is not uncommon, nor is restless sleep with night terrors, awaking at around the witching hour of 3:00 a.m. Some call it "the 3:00 a.m. club." It's a significant time for Christians because our Lord died around 3:00 p.m. on Good Friday, and so the devil, in his demented efforts to flip all God's good gifts upside down, is particularly active at that time. I've gotten accustomed to living with these wakeups and have ceased being spooked. After a few weeks or months, they subside—until another case comes my way. It's just part of the job.

Christians are all living sacrifices (Rom. 12:1) who suffer for the sake of their neighbor in advancing the gospel. And sacrifices always hurt. Anyway, it makes no difference to me whether these middle-of-the-night wakeups are the work of the devil or the Holy Spirit. I always seize them as an opportunity to pray. We prevail over the dark one each time, as Christ victoriously intercedes for us. I tell my kids the same thing: Whenever they wake up scared, they can just tell the devil they belong to Jesus. It works every time.

A good friend of mine shared with me a series of unsettling dreams she had of demonic figures. They'd begun immediately after I'd asked her to pray for a demoniac with whom I was working. I apologized for the demonic harassment that she was now suffering. Yet she replied, "I am not complaining. Actually, I find it inspiring that the devil is threatened by my prayer life." What a refreshing attitude! Christian warriors don't reject the cross but embrace it (Matt. 16:24).

A man who was very familiar with spiritual attack, Martin Luther, allegedly once observed that "when the devil harasses us, then we know ourselves to be in good shape!" After all, suffering demonic attacks while battling beside or on behalf of others is a natural ramification of being members of the body of Christ. The Christian life is always cruciform while it awaits the certain hope of a glory that will only be revealed in Christ's second coming (Rom. 8:18). The beauty of using a chalice in the celebration of Holy Communion is that it symbolizes how we are not a conglomeration of tiny individual cups but are united as one common cup, as, together, we abide in one Christ. "There is one body and one Spirit—just as you were called to the one hope that belongs to your call—one Lord, one faith, one baptism, one God and Father of all, who is over all and through all and in all" (Eph. 4:4–6).

When it comes to the ministry of deliverance, we do our best with what we have and leave the rest in God's mighty and gracious hands. Spiritual war isn't about what we do but who we are. God can most definitely fight every battle on His own. Why He chooses to partner with us is the bigger mystery. I believe it has something to do with teaching us to rely ever so much more on His mercy and strength. Whenever we believe that we are in the center of the battle, we'll discover in hindsight that we were simple observers on the sidelines. Jesus and His holy angels did all the work on our behalf. And so, while living on earth or lying dead in the grave, we can always "rest in peace."

9

ARMORED BY GOD

Whenever we hear the word *war*, the picture of a soldier springs to mind. It's no accident that God describes Christian ministry as engaging in spiritual war. In the kingdom of God are two kinds of soldiers: angels and Christians. Both operate under the command of our Triune God from the headquarters of heaven. I like to envision the angels as air force personnel and Christians as foot soldiers. We have different skill sets and roles, yet together we fight in coordinated efforts against our common enemy, the devil.

Every individual Christian is crucial in the battle we face together. Pastors are unique in the operations. They not only fight but also train. They lead and equip the body for warfare (Eph. 4:12–16). Regardless of whether we are particularly good at carrying out our tasks, we are chosen by the Lord, recruited into His military force.

The most significant wars are invisible ones. They happen in human hearts because of sin. "For we do not wrestle against flesh and blood, but against the rulers, against the authorities, against the cosmic powers over this present darkness, against the spiritual forces of evil in the heavenly places" (Eph. 6:12). When Adam and Eve walked away from God, they caused a catastrophic explosion that disrupted all orders of the universe. Since then, every conceivable relationship is engaged in this war, which will ensue until the end of time. War is the absence of peace. When we walk away from the Lord of Peace, we get war. Jesus said there would be conflict on earth until we get to heaven (Matt. 24:6), because we remain sinners until we die.

Sure, we are justified and forgiven—holy saints. But at the same time, we remain unholy sinners. The proof is in the fact that everyone dies, since the Bible states that "the wages of sin is death" (Rom. 6:23). So the Old Adam and New Adam inside of us—the two opposite beings that we are—continually wage war against each other until we are carried into the kingdom of glory.

In other words, although we are forgiven, we still bear the consequences of sin. You may be acquitted for a crime you committed, but that doesn't mean the damage you caused magically disappears. We broke the world and now live in a mess for which we are responsible. Yet God has not abandoned us. He became human to unite Himself with us and save us from our sins. He makes us who are unholy holy by His blood (Heb. 10:10).

Meanwhile, the devil wants us to remain tangled in our sins and to live out our identity as sinners instead of wrestling the Old Adam to the ground. But before blaming the devil, hear the words of the great Reformer Martin Luther, who apparently once said, "I don't need the devil to tempt me to sin; I do a pretty good job myself." We can't blame the devil for our faults. Yet we need to be aware that he's real and active in our world. Certainly, Jesus conquered the war with sin, death, and the devil at the cross. He is victorious. But until His return, the renegade forces are somewhat free and are hard at work. They've lost the war, but they are sore losers. They've no hope against God's army but plan to do a lot of damage until the final victory parade at the second coming of Christ.

Ready Despite Appearances

But did you know that you're already equipped with everything necessary to fight this war? God loves you too much to leave you to your own devices. Jesus equips you by grace. Physical war is violent and dangerous, and we must be well-trained, armored, and situated alongside other soldiers in order to survive and succeed—and spiritual battle is even messier, our preparations even more essential.

> For though we walk in the flesh, we are not waging war according to the flesh. For the weapons of our warfare are not of the flesh but have divine power to destroy strongholds. We destroy arguments and every lofty opinion raised against the knowledge of God, and take every thought captive to obey Christ. (2 Cor. 10:3–5)

This covert war is more minacious than any modern-day war. The ultimate goal of the enemy is to stop us from getting to heaven by impeding our right relationship with God on earth. How? He seeks to deprive us of the knowledge necessary for missional success.

In the military, information, intelligence, and situational awareness are needed in order to overcome the enemy. At the very least, you need to know who they are, what they want, and how they seek to attain their goals. Well, the devil wants to take us to hell with him. His strategy is to get us to doubt God's Word, which is our main source of critical information.

Adam and Eve's first mistake wasn't disobedience but doubting God's Word. "Did God really say?" the devil asked them (Gen. 3:1 NIV). They doubted that God was their good heavenly Father as they listened to the seducing words of the serpent. "You won't die! God's got it out for you. He's not good. He's afraid of competitors to His power. He's bad. He's a dictator. He's an abuser."

During one exorcism, I found myself starting to unwittingly believe the manipulative words of a demon determined to convince me that it was the victim and God was the slave driver—until I silenced it. God's Word tells us the truth about who He is, what He thinks about us, and who we are in Him. The devil seeks to undermine that message by lies that lead to death.

God's Word is powerful. With His Word, He created the world out of nothing. With His Word, He creates faith out of nothing. With His Word, He sustains that very same saving faith. The forces of hell are terrified of those divine words, as the evil hosts are destined to one day bow their knees in subjection to the Word made flesh (Phil. 2:10–11). Yet the enemy's words are also powerful if you allow yourself to believe them. The serpent's lies can kill your faith as you become collateral damage in the cosmic battle.

All false teaching consists of lies about God and about your relationship with Him. Through those lies, Satan seeks to lead you into despair or self-righteousness. He wants you to doubt your total dependence upon your almighty and loving Lord and tempts you to question that He has already achieved everything you need to overcome your spiritual enemies. For instance, Lucifer wants you to doubt the heavenly citizenship that already belongs to you in Christ. For "our citizenship is in heaven, and from it we await a Savior, the Lord Jesus Christ, who will transform our lowly body to be like his glorious body, by the power that enables him even to subject all things to himself" (Phil. 3:20–21).

Now imagine you're a tourist visiting a developing country that abruptly enters into a civil war. You race to the airport in hopes of catching the next flight out. Your only hope is in the fact that you are an American citizen. And then someone gets you to doubt your citizenship or claims that your passport is a forgery! Wouldn't that be terrible? What hope would you have to be saved?

We have salvation from the spiritual wars around us through Jesus Christ and His cross because we are citizens of this King's country. In fact, we're not only citizens but children adopted into a divinely royal family. When you were baptized, you received that citizenship with a legitimate passport signed by the blood of Christ. You were snatched out of the kingdom of the evil enemy and given the rights of a heavenly child. Of course, you can't see it. You live by faith.

Well, the devil, the secular world, and your old self like to get you to doubt that. They want you to believe that the passport you received in your baptism, bought by Jesus on the cross, isn't sufficient. They want you to trust your eyes, experiences, feelings, and emotions. The fact that you don't live up to the standards of this citizenship, or that you don't feel the Spirit's presence in your life, can often make a compelling argument that you don't belong to the Lord.

Yet by trusting in the forgiveness of sins and the grace of Christ—something you don't deserve or earn by your good works and behavior—you're able to press through those lies and rejoice in your status as citizen and child. Whether you feel it or not, you are God's child. This good news is so wonderful that it motivates you to try better to live up to your reputation as God's child by seeking to please Him through obeying His holy commandments.

Innumerable privileges come with heavenly citizenship. Our loving God generously showers gifts upon His children well before the full inheritance is shared. So it's no surprise that God has equipped us properly for the battle as His holy soldiers. He's given us all we need to get to heaven where we'll enjoy the inheritance He can't wait to grant us there.

Ephesians 6:10–17

One of the chief passages that unpacks this comforting truth about the fundamental armor that already belongs to us is recorded in St. Paul's letter to the Ephesians:

> Finally, be strengthened in the Lord, that is, in his mighty strength. Let yourselves be clothed with the full armor of God so that you may be able to stand against the devil's schemes. For our struggle is not against blood and flesh, but against the rulers, against the authorities, against the world powers of this darkness, against the spiritual forces of evil in the heavenly places. For this reason take up the full armor of God, that you may be able to withstand in the evil day, and so, having accomplished all things, to stand. Stand, therefore, having belted your waist with truth, and having clothed yourself with the breastplate of righteousness, and having shod your feet with the preparation of the Gospel of peace, among all these things having taken up the shield of faith, with which you will be able to extinguish all the flaming arrows of the evil one; and receive the helmet of salvation, and the short sword of the Spirit, which is the Word of God. (Eph. 6:10–17)[1]

1. Thomas M. Winger, *Ephesians*, Concordia Commentary Series (Concordia Publishing House, 2015), 699.

I adopted the above translation from a colleague of mine who is an expert scholar on St. Paul's letter to the Ephesians. Most translations imply that spiritual warfare involves a lot of doing on our part, whereas the original language underscores how we're passive recipients of God's gifts. Instead of the *prescriptive* language "clothe yourself"—which makes Christians feel they must do something to equip themselves—this passage more accurately *describes* the Christian state, encouraging soldiers to continue being what they already are and receiving what is already theirs. "Be clothed" suggests a passive reception of the equipment of God. God wants us to take what we have been given. Instead of resisting and struggling against the ways in which He dresses us, Christians are to simply submit in faith to the act of God. When it comes to spiritual armor, our job is holding on to what God has given us and guarding it with our lives.

After all, we don't make ourselves strong. We are made strong. Jesus compares Christians with children, even babies (Matt. 18:3), to humble our adultlike patterns of thinking that search for strength, power, and wisdom from *within*. Babies are helpless. They can't even put on their own clothes. They rely on others. In the kingdom of God, those who see themselves as tiny babies make the most powerful soldiers!

Already Equipped

When new soldiers sign their name on the dotted line at the military recruitment center, they get everything they need to carry out their new vocation right away. But they still need to be trained to use the gear rightly. It also takes some getting used to—adjusting the strap on the helmet, finding the safety on the gun, and so on. That's how it is with us Christian soldiers. God has given us all we need, and His equipment works perfectly well, but we still need training.

In the fictional world of C. S. Lewis's Narnia, the children receive their gifts from the Christ figure, Aslan, by grace. The great lion equips them. Yet he explains the gear to them and instructs them on how it is to be used. Then he clothes them with it. They do nothing. They just receive. The children are astonished at how efficacious the weapons are, in spite of their inexperience: Lucy's potion, Susan's bow, and Peter's sword are all powerful in themselves. The weak and unskilled children rejoice with amazement as to how well they can fight the white witch's beasts. Clearly, none of the victories can be attributed to themselves. The gifts do all the work. Likewise, we Christians use what we've been given, and it works all by itself . . . almost. Babies aren't good at doing much—except one thing. Trusting. And so *that* is the secret ingredient when it comes to spiritual battle!

"Be strengthened in the Lord, that is, in his mighty strength."[2] Focusing on your own spiritual force or power will always disappoint. For those who are completely honest with themselves, it will lead to despair, which is exactly what the devil wants. He aims to make you feel like the battle will be won or lost based on what you *do*, instead of what Christ has already *done*.

True Christianity won't lure you into an existential quest in search of internal spiritual strength and personal meaning, as is the case with false religions. You've already received everything necessary at baptism. You have your identity in Christ. That includes your vocation as a soldier. And your divine commander is so committed to your success that He's given you all His armor to get the job done well. He earned it. He made it. He tested it at the cross. He has clothed you with it. Knowing that is the first step in using it. Because of

2. Winger, *Ephesians*, 699.

Him, the armor does the fighting for you, and you practically do nothing, besides letting it happen and rejoicing in the outcome. You trust the workings of the equipment and results of the battle into the hefty hands of God. That's faith.

Yet still, we have a hard time believing that this foreign armor we wear and the weapons we handle are as reliable as we're told. I remember an army friend once musing, "Chaplain, when it comes to the devil and spiritual war, we are all just little vulnerable babies. We've got nothing going for us. Except this: we've each got our hands on a missile. The Word of God! The enemy isn't afraid of the baby, but he is terrified of the gun. Our problem is, we don't realize that we aren't just holding a toy."

We often act in ways that trivialize the significance of the gear with which we've been vested. We have unimaginable power to influence the trajectory that evil events crave to take at our fingertips: folded in morning prayer at our bedside, flipping through pages of the Holy Scriptures in our study space, or grasping a chalice of consecrated wine at Sunday morning mass. For here are some of the places that God keeps our armor polished, outfitted for battle with His state-of-the-art equipment in carrying out His divine mission: saving sinners by snatching them from hell's fire (Jude 23).

When St. Paul says, "Let yourselves be clothed with the full armor of God,"[3] he uses a divine passive form of the verb to emphasize that we are simply the receptors of another's gear. What's our role in putting it on? Simply letting it be done. But that's harder than it sounds. Have you ever tried dressing a child who thinks they are old enough to do it all by themselves, even though they aren't? That's our problem. God does it all. Yet we get in the way. Like stubborn little

3. Winger, *Ephesians*, 699.

children who think they're in charge, we wiggle and squirm. Our pride makes everything unnecessarily difficult. We remain saved by grace. But it's a lot of work remembering that we are passive recipients of all of God's gifts; that *our* clothing is *His* righteousness.

Here's another way of thinking about it. When I served overseas, one of the safest places to be in the battlefield was in an armored vehicle. While you're in a tank, it's pretty evident how small and weak you are as the machine protects you and fights for you. And from this safe and secure position, soldiers simply watch the victory unfold through a tiny little window slot. In the tank of His Holy Church, dressed in the clothing of Christ, we don't fight for God. Rather, He fights for us! Like a loving Father who is willing to lay down His life for His children, He defends us from our enemies. The Bible records countless examples of how "human" victory is in reality God's triumph.

When the servant of the prophet Elisha watches a massive enemy army approaching, he runs to the man of God in hysteria. What's Elisha's response? He prays, "'O LORD, please open his eyes that he may see.' So the LORD opened the eyes of the young man, and he saw, and behold, the mountain was full of horses and chariots of fire all around Elisha" (2 Kings 6:17).

We shouldn't trust our eyes or feelings in judging spiritual conquests. We may look defeated. We may feel like losers. Yet God is there, and the triumph is already ours. And yet we still doubt.

Even David, God's faithful servant, gave in to the temptation to trust in his own strength, wealth, and glory for victory. "Then Satan stood against Israel and incited David to number Israel" (1 Chron. 21:1) as a way of persuading the king to rely on his huge number of soldiers and people instead of God. David's pride and ego fed his desire for earthly glory. God was not pleased. David's flickering faith led him to count the numbers. This resulted in great calamity.

God wants to be our strength. He alone is able. He wants to rid us of anxiety and doubt in His providence and goodness. We are to rest in Him alone. In fact, the smaller and weaker we look or feel, the greater opportunity God has to show His greatness. "God chose what is weak in the world to shame the strong" (1 Cor. 1:27).

Remember this the next time you are tempted to judge the success of your church based on its size or number of attendees: The church at Calvary consisted of one bloody man hanging on a lonely cross with a few lowly followers weeping at its foot, sprinkled with the blood of God. Nobody felt good about themselves. The triumph was a hidden phenomenon. That is a picture of the true Church, and the devil trembles in trepidation at the thought of it (James 2:19).

Standing Firm

"Stand." "Don't move." There are all kinds of soldiers, but in Ephesians 6, St. Paul has one type in mind. What kind of soldiers just stand guard and don't move? Not infantry, but sentries. Remember, when St. Paul is writing this epistle, he's in prison and is surrounded by Roman guards who stay put in one place. Paul compares us Christians with that kind of soldier. We practice *defensive* warfare. So he repeats the word *stand* several times. Don't go looking for action but responsibly address it when it finds you. True warriors of faith courageously stand in the grace of God (Rom. 5:2), relying on divine might and a timing that is not their own.

The greatest error a soldier can make is aspiring to be the hero, such as an aggressive Rambo-like individualist, trigger-happy and looking for a fight. We've already talked about the danger of being a ghost hunter, chasing demons out of curiosity or with a macho attitude. They're weak in faith and immature. They've become restless with the role assigned to them by God. They have their own battles into which God has sent them. It's dangerous business engaging in combats to which God hasn't assigned you. Humble servants don't go looking for trouble but stay put in their place until trouble finds them. Moreover, consider that if a Roman sentry left his post or fell asleep (i.e., stopped "standing"), he would be executed for treason. Now, our merciful Lord forgives us for our failures, just as He did for the disciples who slept while guarding our Lord in the garden of Gethsemane. Still, Paul's comparison of Christian warriors and sentry guards acts as a critical reminder to us that our standing on guard for Christ and the truth is not to be taken lightly.

The chain of command carefully positions soldiers in specific places and for reasons to which they are not always privy. So, too, in the kingdom of God we pray, "Thy will be done." Admittedly, the soldier may not agree with, understand, or like the decision. Tough luck! We don't belong to ourselves but to the Lord. We're called to guard the posts at which the Lord has placed us and not abandon them at any cost, even when our callings seem ordinary, boring, and "unspiritual." Each one of our many vocations in life is essential. Whether we're parent or child, employee or employer, leader or follower, the Holy Scriptures clearly indicate what services are required of us.

God has placed you where you are as His soldier. When trouble comes, you defend your position. Good soldiers don't go running away from their post like cowards or fall asleep on the job. God's brought certain people into your life and given you a unique set of jobs, gifts, and talents for fulfilling your role in serving them. Obedient Christian servants accept their God-given gifts and cherish them.

All our vocations demand that we stand firm in the Faith and speak the truth from within them, in the estates of family, Church, and state. David was hunted down by the murderous tyrant Saul for simply obeying God's Word. The prophet Zechariah was stoned to death in the temple court-yard for condemning both civil and ecclesiastical authorities for their rebellion against God. John the Baptist was be-headed for confronting government abuse and immorality. "Woe to you, when all people speak well of you, for so their fathers did to the false prophets" (Luke 6:26). Sometimes our work includes tremendously heavy crosses. Yet we pick them up and carry on, even unto death.

God put you where you are, so just stand there. React to what life throws at you, entrusting it all into the hands of a good, gracious, and omniscient God, just like a little help-less baby does when happily resting in his or her mother's arms. Only then are you able to "rejoice always, pray without ceasing, [and] give thanks in all circumstances" (1 Thess. 5:16–18).

Wearing the Clothing of Christ

Belt

"Stand, therefore, having belted your waist with truth."[4] We don't usually think of a belt as an important piece of clothing, but for Roman soldiers it didn't just hold up their pants. It was vital not only for affixing the sword but also in binding the entire uniform. Without it, a soldier would trip over his long Roman robes. In the army today, the tactical

4. Winger, *Ephesians*, 699.

vest is requisite to holding all the gear tightly together and close to the body.

Your belt is "truth." Christians are belted by true doctrine, especially the message that Jesus is "the way, and the truth, and the life. No one comes to the Father except through [Him]" (John 14:6). Reciting, confessing, and praying historical creeds help keep that belt tight. The truth about Jesus unifies all the parts of your gear and is the very reason for which you are geared up.

The belt also marked the vocation of the soldier. Today's elite special operations forces often bear a special emblem on their belts, indicating the specialization of the unit to which they belong. In the regular forces, rank and vocation are often displayed by a badge on the tactical vest. It all amounts to the same thing: a reminder to both you and others of who you are. It's a warning to your enemy, and it's a morale boost to yourself, recalling that you belong to Jesus the Christ and fight under the sign of His holy cross.

Breastplate

"Stand, therefore . . . having clothed yourself with the breastplate of righteousness."[5] What does a breastplate do? It shields the heart. In the military today, an "anti-frag vest" functions in the same way. These steel plates are heavy, so you never forget they are there.

The righteousness of God shields the Christian heart. No one is righteous in themselves. We are all sinners. Instead, "for our sake he made him to be sin who knew no sin, so that in him we might become the righteousness of God" (2 Cor. 5:21). In other words, you are righteous before God and holy in His sight for Christ's sake. Jesus covers your

5. Winger, *Ephesians*, 699.

sinful and unrighteous nakedness with His perfect robe of righteousness. Being covered by the blood of the Lamb is identical to being wrapped in this divine garb (Rev. 7:14). The newly baptized often wear a white gown or towel, symbolizing this important truth. You are geared in Christ's armor, purchased and won for you at the cross and given to you at your baptism. And God makes good stuff!

Shoes

"Stand, therefore . . . having shod your feet with the Gospel of peace."[6] You respond to danger by moving your feet. And the shoes of the Christian are the gospel: "How beautiful upon the mountains are the feet of him who brings good news, who publishes peace" (Isa. 52:7). As Christians, we are messengers of the gospel. Christians fight with love against our enemies, turning the other cheek and doing good to those who seek to do us harm. It's a perplexing battle without parallel in the world in which we stand.

When we're honest, we admit that we don't like this. We'd rather seek victory ourselves, visible triumphs attuned to the ways of the world. We want to think of ourselves as unassailable warriors. We wish to witness demons groveling before us, begging for mercy. We desire to see our enemies punished, and we invent or imagine clever ways of taking revenge on those who mistreat us, tit for tat. So the Word reminds us that we are representatives of the kingdom of heaven on earth. We are ambassadors from a different land. We wear the uniform of a spiritual nation. We behave as citizens of heaven. Following Christ's Word, we practice self-control and gentleness. We are chivalrous knights who ultimately seek everlasting peace.

6. Winger, *Ephesians*, 699.

That's why it's only when you surrender yourself to the Holy Spirit at the foot of the cross, in daily repentance, that you can effectively fight in the strength of the Lord, defend yourself with divine wisdom, and advance the kingdom with the gospel of peace. Your tactics involve love, grace, forgiveness, and kindness. Amid the universal cosmic war between God and the devil, Jesus pleads, "Father, forgive them, for they know not what they do" (Luke 23:34). He responds with patient love and gentle prayer. St. Stephen mimics this behavior when he is stoned to death for standing against the devilish enemies of Christ. "And falling to his knees he cried out with a loud voice, 'Lord, do not hold this sin against them'" (Acts 7:60). What is the lesson for us? "Do not be overcome by evil, but overcome evil with good" (Rom. 12:21).

When you react professionally to demonic forces, responding with a humble faith in God and sincere love for your human enemy, you "heap burning coals on his head, and the LORD will reward you" (Prov. 25:22). The way Christians battle is unique, which is why we are ridiculed by unbelievers. But deep down, those who jeer at us are jealous and dumbfounded by our tactics. Some are driven to the Lord in their search for an alternative to the nihilism so prevalent in the world around them. When we resort to the world's ways of fighting, we get in the way of the *missio dei*.

When King Jehoshaphat of Judah panicked at the sight of the devilish enemy armies, the Lord's prophet consoled him and the people, saying,

> "You will not need to fight in this battle. Stand firm, hold your position, and see the salvation of the LORD on your behalf, O Judah and Jerusalem." Do not be afraid and do not be dismayed. Tomorrow go out against them, and the LORD will be with you. (2 Chron. 20:17)

194

Because they believed, they obeyed. They didn't behave like a regular army. All they did was praise God for His love, singing, "Give thanks to the LORD, for his steadfast love endures forever" (v. 21). God delivered them. This is a picture of the Church.

Shield

"Stand, therefore . . . having taken the shield of faith to extinguish fiery arrows of the evil one."[7] The two items that move on the body of a guard are the sword and the shield. Their location changes to suit the situation. For Christian soldiers, faith governs adaptation to each changing environment.

As mentioned earlier, the Church talks about faith in two ways: *fides qua* (personal trust) and *fides quae* (communal confession of a shared belief). A Christian professes, "*I* believe in Jesus as my Savior," as well as "*We* believe the Christian Faith." Both personal faith and communal confession of the one true Faith are necessary for success in this battle. Without a right knowledge and a full understanding of the Church's infallible doctrine (when it stems from the Holy Scriptures), invoking the name of Jesus makes no sense.

Some purported followers of our Lord will cast out demons in Jesus's holy name and yet hear Him declare, "I never knew you" (Matt. 7:23). One can't insist on having love for Jesus while having little knowledge about His attributes, lacking a basic ability to speak about His two natures as both God and man, or not caring about how He relates to the Father and Holy Spirit in the Holy Trinity. A commitment to studying the doctrines of the Bible in depth is mandatory for a serious Christian. At the same time, one can adhere

---

7. Winger, *Ephesians*, 699.

to all the right orthodox teachings of the Faith but lack a sincere belief in them. Such people don't have an authentic living personal faith.

Soldiers in this battle are shaped and formed by both "head" and "heart" kinds of faith. When you are tempted, you need to trust fully in Jesus to extinguish the fiery darts of the evil one. When the devil lies to you through the mouth of a demoniac (and the devil knows the Bible through and through!), you extinguish those fiery darts by responding theologically. We Christians may often feel like we're on the losing side. That's why we walk by faith and not by sight, trusting in God's Word. Our eyes, hearts, and experiences will often deceive us. But God's promises never will. *Fides quae* confesses those promises. *Fides qua* holds on to them.

Often it seems that many Christians don't experience persecution or trials in their soldiering. Outside of ordinary temptations in their hearts, they don't appear to suffer the same kinds of attacks from the world or the devil as others. Those who don't have the courage to open their mouths, stand up for the truth, challenge injustice, or turn to prayer immediately when trouble arrives (instead of as a last resort) don't pose a serious threat to the kingdom of darkness. Accordingly, they won't suffer persecution. They have fled from their post. If the devil doesn't consider you a threat, he'll likely leave you alone. But when you speak out, "in season and out of season" (2 Tim. 4:2), and are active defending the Faith, boldly proclaiming the truth, rebuking false doctrine, and preaching the gospel without compromise, get ready for enemy attack. The devil will pull out the big guns. But don't run. Consider yourself blessed, deemed worthy to matter in the fight.

God will never give you more than you can handle. If you get led into this kind of ministry, it's because God wants you there. He chose you. "God is faithful, and he will not let you be tempted beyond your ability" (1 Cor. 10:13), for what others intend for evil, even when it comes to the devil and his evil designs on you, God will turn to good (Gen. 50:20). Besides, it's an honor to suffer. "Share in suffering as a good soldier of Christ Jesus" (2 Tim. 2:3). Soldiers take pride in their scars and war wounds. Such Christians join St. Paul in his declaration: "I bear on my body the marks of Jesus" (Gal. 6:17).

Helmet

"Receive the helmet of salvation."[8] What are the two most important body parts to protect in a battle? The head and the heart: what you believe *in* your head and *with* your heart. "If you confess with your mouth that Jesus is Lord and believe in your heart that God raised him from the dead, you will be saved" (Rom. 10:9). But like any gift or tool, you can choose to toss it aside. If you neglect to care for your armor, it will rust. If you don't value or use it, it will lose its effectiveness.

How does this happen? By becoming a lazy, lukewarm warrior. On the one hand, Christians are passive recipients of salvation—saved by grace alone. But on the other hand, we're not to resist the work of the Holy Spirit in our lives or become lax in the battle of faith (Eph. 4:30; 1 Thess. 5:19). The fact that God justifies and sanctifies us all by Himself doesn't mean we have no role to play in spiritual warfare.

Being a soldier takes work, education, and training. Soldiers are characterized by discipline. They work out daily. They eat well. They zero in on the mission. They don't run away from danger, suffering, or pain: "Share in suffering as a good soldier of Christ Jesus . . . [whose] aim is to please

8. Winger, *Ephesians*, 699.

the one who enlisted him" (2 Tim. 2:3–4). They're models for us to follow.

You've been given the armor of God as a gift, one that takes upkeep and attracts a lot of nasty attention from the enemy. As I already mentioned, we're like small children who don't want to be dressed by another, thinking we can do it better ourselves. God wants us to be still and let Him do it. You maintain your armor by exposing yourself continually to the gospel Word and the sacraments. In that way, Jesus keeps it clean, polished, oiled, and "good to go." The blood of Jesus keeps you strong and wise.

Also, a soldier's armor needs constant tightening and inspection by other Christians. When I served with the paratroopers, before every jump from an airplane, my partners would check my gear for safety. Your pastor and other Christians do the same for you through the life of the Church and God-pleasing worship. Spiritual war is often a team effort. God uses the Church, and especially His pastors, to keep up the training and the maintenance of His holy armor.

When the Narnian children see how powerful their weapons are, they don't need any prodding to put them to good use. As God's saints, soldiers, and athletes, we discipline ourselves not because we must but because we want to.

Sword

"And [receive] the short sword of the Spirit, which is the Word of God."[9] We now come to the only piece of equipment for *offensive* warfare. It's a short sword because, for sentries, an enemy attack is a one-on-one, close contact battle. Even today, most soldiers carry a knife for hand-to-hand combat.

9. Winger, *Ephesians*, 699.

When Jesus fought Satan in the desert, He kept His words with the devil short and to a minimum. Jesus just quoted a few Scriptures that chase the evil one away. Christ is an example for us, but He's even more. Because He is the unique Son of God, every divine word has its power in Him. Jesus is literally present in His word. What an amazing comfort when we feel alone.

Christian battles with the devil are often intimate, happening in the deep and secret recesses of our hearts and souls. Nobody but God can really understand those intense struggles. And in those moments, when we respond with the Word of God (Matt. 4:1–11) and prayer, we thrust the short sword into the gut of the insidious foe. He "shudders" when he hears this Word (James 2:19). Like David facing off with Goliath, one small stone topples the evil giant to the ground.

Memorizing God's Word and Christian hymns is a guaranteed way of having a sharpened sword, or ammunition in the barrel, ready to go. Some churches have catechisms that summarize Christian doctrine, providing an easy way to memorize Holy Scripture. In many biblically based traditional churches, believers hear the same liturgy sung or spoken week after week. Because these services consist largely of Scripture passages, worshipers are memorizing the Bible every time they attend worship services.

Imagine being a soldier on patrol with a gun—but it's not loaded. The moment the enemy attacks, you cry out, "Hold on a second while I load this thing! Hmmm. How does this thing work? Where's the manual?" The Word of God is like ammunition. Every soldier naturally wants to be prepared with a tight grip on their gun. Memorizing the Word keeps you ready to use it. Repeating it to yourself out loud or in your head when you are having a bad day, sharing it with a friend who needs godly advice, or even telling a random stranger about Jesus are just a few examples of swinging the sword of the Spirit or firing that gun.

I know a lot of Christians who have fallen from the Faith due to sloppy battling by neglecting their armor and forgetting how to use their weapons. But with eyes fixed on the cross of your Lord, you never have a reason to fear, and you always have a pathway back.

No, in all these things we are more than conquerors through him who loved us. For I am sure that neither death nor life, nor angels nor rulers, nor things present nor things to come, nor powers, nor height nor depth, nor anything else in all creation, will be able to separate us from the love of God in Christ Jesus our Lord. (Rom. 8:37–39)

CONCLUSION

Never Be Discouraged: Christ Is Always There

Christ, the Lord of hosts, unshaken
By the devil's seething rage,
Thwarts the plan of Satan's minions;
Wins the strife from age to age;
Conquers sin and death forever;
Slams them in their steely cage.[1]

So go the poetic and potent words of a modern hymn designated for Michaelmas—the feast day of St. Michael and all angels—on September 29. It also happens to be the day I first exorcised a demon out of Frank, the troubled man I discussed in the introduction. At least on one day of the year, we recall how Jesus, who conquered the devil on that first Good Friday and Easter Sunday, continues to fight spiritual battles on our behalf. But if you're anything like me, you need that reminder every day.

Every Christian is by nature a spiritual warrior serving in a kingdom that is assaulted daily by devilish enemies. We

1. Peter M. Prange, "Christ, the Lord of Hosts, Unshaken," *Lutheran Service Book*, 521.

know we need to be prepared for countless temptations by the devil. Yet many of the kinds of devilish attacks discussed in this book aren't common occurrences for the average person. Preparing for the ministry of deliverance won't be intuitive. To complicate matters, little credible material has been written on the subject. And yet, determining the kind and degree of demonic presence, and the steps involved in a responsible response, requires some instruction. Otherwise, we tend to understate or overstate the problem. This is why I've tried to provide some training, advice, and guidelines in this book, even though there's much more that can be said.

As a young boy, I had recurring nightmares of being trapped in a haunted house and chased around by a demon. Right before being overtaken by this monster, I would wake up in a cold sweat. As I matured in my faith, I began to rebuke this creature in the name of Jesus. I would swing my sword in my dream and defeat it. The same tools we use while awake are also effective while asleep. We are most vulnerable to the darkness after we close our eyes. This is why the prayer of the ancient Compline rite, with origins stretching back to the second century, continues to be used by Christian families and communities before bed: "Guide us waking, O Lord, and guard us sleeping; that awake we may watch with Christ, and asleep we may rest in peace."[2]

The Christian toolbox, handed down to each one of us through the historical Church, has stood the test of time. It's filled with lots of equipment that has often been overlooked. But once rediscovered, these tools become indispensable helps in the Christian life.

When it comes to the ministry of deliverance, we're best equipped for the extraordinary when our weapons are well

2. *Lutheran Service Book*, 258.

maintained and in good shape thanks to our ordinary day-to-day battles with evil. Supernatural battles are revealed in demonism, but don't be fooled. Though normally concealed, they happen every day in each Christian heart. We just don't see it, which is why we should never trust our eyes.

Physical manifestations of the devil are real. This fact can't be emphasized too strongly. If you don't believe that by now, then reading this book was largely a waste of your time. But if you're a Christian, then be convinced that you can unknowingly entertain angels that appear to you in physical ways, disguised as humans (Heb. 13:2). The reverse holds true as well.

Rationalism inevitably impacts exegesis. The earliest Old Testament commentators believed in real monstrous giants and supernatural creatures based on literal interpretations of the text. For example, the Nephilim of the perverted generation prior to the great flood were understood as offspring of fallen angels that had procreated with women (Gen. 6:4; Num. 13:33). Modern Western scholars tend to interpret all these figures spiritually. Yet when you've seen what I have, you become open-minded to all sorts of bizarre, even apparently outlandish hypotheses. A woman from Sweden once reached out to me for help. Among the list of demonic attacks on her body was repeated rape by an invisible entity. But before judging such allegations too harshly, remember that the most preposterous supernatural idea is that God has become human—fully divine and fully human, two opposites in one joined together forever, present invisibly but physically everywhere in the universe (Eph. 1:23), making Himself accessible to us in the Holy Supper of His body and blood, where He incorporates us into Himself forever. And He does it all because He loves us. The message of Christianity is as impossible to believe as any claim of demonic "incarnation," which is why faith is a gift of the Holy Spirit (Rom. 10:17).

Don't let the philosophy of rationalism poison your ability to discern things spiritually. When you let skepticism get you to doubt the devil's presence, before you know it, you'll also be doubting God's. At the same time, be careful not to overdo it by mistaking the regular temptations and darknesses of life with demonism. Only after you've carefully determined that more is going on in a person's life or home than meets the eye, through asking some tough and uncomfortable questions, can your suspicions of demonic presence be reasonably confirmed.

Your pastor, and not a psychologist, should be your first stop. Sadly, many pastors are skeptical or cowardly, hiding from the unknown, even though delivering hurting and helpless people from the grip of darkness is ultimately the heart of the Christian mission. Still, God is good, and He provides.

Through personal anecdotes, biblical narratives, and plain and simple reason, this book has been preparing you for once rare yet now increasing demonic encounters. I believe demonic oppression and possession will become more common for generations to come in North America, based on current religious, cultural, and political trends in society. Christians will be offered new chances to "be relevant" in a darkening, secular world that has little knowledge of the true Faith and is desperate for answers and help. Maneuvering responsibly within these frightening yet exciting times—which, when it comes to theological considerations and caregiving implications, can sometimes feel like a boundless minefield—involves ensuring that we are clothed by Christ and His armor, positioned behind Him, and actively battling our enemies with the Word, prayer, and humility.

Yet have no fear. When the disciples were shaking with fright in their homes on that first Easter morning, or when petrified by the waves of the storm that threatened to engulf their boat, or terrified by supernatural experiences of angelic visits, our Lord appeared in their midst with fatherly and comforting words like: "Do not be afraid" (Matt. 28:5). Jesus still consoles us today. We have no reason to fear (1 John 4:18) because "[we have been] rescued from the lion's mouth. The Lord will rescue [us] from every evil deed and bring [us] safely into his heavenly kingdom. To him be the glory forever and ever. Amen" (2 Tim. 4:17–18).

We've been equipped and sent by our Lord, who has already achieved the victory. Yet we don't just sit still. We fight. And the best way to fight is not with our fists but on our knees.

Lord, teach us to pray.

> *Jesus, send Your angel legions*
> *When the foe would us enslave*
> *Hold us fast when sin assaults us;*
> *Come, then, Lord, Your people save.*
> *Overthrow at last the dragon;*
> *Send him to his fiery grave.*[3]

3. Prange, "Christ, the Lord of Hosts, Unshaken."

205

ABOUT THE AUTHOR

Harold Ristau was born in Waterloo, Ontario, Canada, and has served as a parish pastor, military chaplain, African missionary, and seminary professor. He is currently the president of Luther Classical College in Casper, Wyoming. He holds a BA and MA in political science and economics, with specialties in administrative studies (University of Waterloo), an MDiv (Brock University), and a PhD in religious studies (McGill University). He is the author of several publications on a vast array of political, ethical, and theological subjects and the author of several books including *My First Exorcism: What the Devil Taught a Lutheran Pastor About Counter-Cultural Spirituality*, *When You Fast: The Sacramental Character of Fasting*, *At Peace with War: A Chaplain's Meditations from Afghanistan*, and *Spiritual Warfare: For the Care of Souls*. He is married with five children and one grandchild.